Uncovering the Demigods

Discover the Superhumans From Greek, Norse, Celtic, African, Egyptian, Japanese, and Hindu Mythology

Lucas Russo

losses, direct or indirect, that are incurred as a result of the use of the information contained within this document, including, but not limited to, errors, omissions,orinac curacies.

Table of Contents

Introduction

Demigods—who are they? If you've ever participated in modern culture, you might know names such as Hercules or Achilles, but you might not have heard their stories to the full extent. Or maybe you are a Percy Jackson fan, and you have seen many demigods on your movie screen—or on the pages of your books. Or you might be a Marvel enthusiast and don't yet realize how many things the modern superheroes have in common with the demigods from various mythological traditions.

In the simplest sense of the word, a demigod is someone conceived from a union between a god and a human. So far, so simple: Hercules—or, as the Greeks called him, Heracles—was the son of the king of gods, Zeus, and a human woman named Alcmene. Because of that, he was supernaturally strong and capable of performing the deeds that would be impossible for simple mortals—and yet, he could still die, and indeed he did, even if he was taken to Olympus after his death.

But what about notable humans who have been, out of gratitude and veneration, deified after their death? Can they be classified as demigods too? Some of them were semi legendary characters, but others were historical figures—such as the Egyptian pharaohs. And what about all those kings and queens who claimed they were the descendants of the gods in order to legitimize their rule?

As you can probably see, the category of a demigod is already becoming a bit murkier. Add to that all the differences between the nature of various mythologies across the world, and you'll have quite an intriguing and not at all straightforward picture. Why were some mythologies practically obsessed with demigod-like figures, while others only seem to have one or two of them? Those questions don't have one simple answer, but I will attempt to give some explanations in the subsequent chapters of this book.

So, without further ado, get ready for a journey of epic proportions. This time, I won't just take you to one mythological tradition. We will meet demigods from multiple cultures, from Greek, Norse, and Celtic, through African, Egyptian, Japanese, and Hindu—to other, perhaps lesser-known traditions such as Mesopotamian, Assyrian, and Polynesian. You will learn the original stories behind the characters popular in modern-day culture, but perhaps even more importantly, you will meet fascinating heroes of whom you might not have heard before. Many of them, quite unjustly, have either been forgotten or are not too well-known to Western audiences. Some of them will be demigods in the simplest meaning of the word, others—deified mortals. Not all of them will be men. So buckle up and be ready to be swept into an adventure of epic proportions, into many worlds in which heroes can defeat armies, change weather, or advance civilizations—while all the time remaining relatable to us mere mortals, sometimes even painfully so.Aft er all, they are always at least part-human.

Chapter 1:

Greek Mythology

The world of Greek demigods is perhaps the one best known to modern Western audiences. Who hasn't heard of Hercules? But the Greek tradition is so much more than that. The Greeks loved their demigod figures, an intrinsic part of their mythology being that Zeus—and other gods—were chasing human women left and right. From numerous dalliances of the king of the gods with those chosen mortals, countless demigods were born, and I will not tell the stories of each and every one of them, instead focusing on the most extensive and interesting tales. Some sons of Zeus were rather straightforward heroes—such as Perseus, who decapitated a beastly woman, Medusa, and saved Princess Andromeda from a sea monster in a very classic princess-and-the-dragon fashion—while others were more tragic figures, such as Tantalus, who was cruelly punished by the gods for the theft of ambrosia, the food of the immortals. But other demigods—and it's their stories that I will focus on in this chapter—are less easily classifiable as simply heroes or villains. Both Heracles and Achilles have triumph and tragedy written into their stories, and both Hippolyta and Helen of Spartaare ve nerated as well as cursed.

The Story of Heracles

The Childhood of a Hero

The name Hercules, which we mostly associate with the famous Greek hero and demigod, is a Romanized version of the Greek name Heracles. But it wasn't the name of our hero from the start: When he was born from an affair between Zeus and Alcmene, a human woman who is sometimes credited with being a descendant of Perseus, he was given the name Alcides. It was subsequently changed to Heracles, meaning "Hera's pride," in order to pacify Zeus's jealous and inconsolable wife. The motif of Hera being jealous of Zeus's affairs and tormenting humans born of them is common in Greek mythology, but in the story of Heracles, it becomese specially prominent.

All attempts at pacifying Hera proved fruitless; soon, when the little Heracles was only 2 months old, the wrathful goddess sent venomous snakes to attack him and his human-born twin brother, Iphicles. But when Iphicles cried out in fear, Heracles grabbed the snakes by their necks and strangled them. Completely unfazed by the danger posed by the creatures, he then proceeded to play with them—and thus, he was found by his nurse. This extraordinary deed would become the first famous exploit of Heracles and would give way to many depictions of him as a child playing with snakes. It would also be a prophecy: Heracles was to destroy many mythical creatures as a grown man, just as he killedt he snakes as a baby.

First Marriage and the Stroke of Tragedy

While still a young man, Heracles traveled to Thebes. It was then ruled by a legendary king, Creon, who welcomed the already renowned hero with open arms. Heracles helped the king in leading the defense against the group of people known as the Minyans, who had been harassing Thebes repeatedly in the past. He won Creon a victory and, as a reward, was allowed to marry the king's daughter, Megara. The couple had three sons, ande verything suggests that they were happy together.

But Hera was still set on ruining Heracles' life. She sent a divinely induced fit of madness on him, during which he threw his sons into a fire and, in the end, also killed Megara. It's hard to imagine what must have gone on in Heracles' heart when the fit finally passed. Horrified at what he had done, he fled to one of the most important places in the ancient Greek world: the oracle at Delphi.

The oracle, whose instructions were treated as the words of the god Apollo himself, ordered Heracles to go to Argos near his family home and offer himself in servitude to King Eurystheus.

Incidentally, Eurystheus was Heracles' cousin and archenemy. Born on the same night as Heracles, he had been favored by Hera who, in order to prevent Heracles from inheriting the kingdom of Argos, hastened Eurystheus' birth, which gave him precedence inhisc laimt ot he throne.

But unlike Heracles with his bravery and strength, Eurystheus was cowardly and scheming. He was more than happy to accept his cousin's offer of servitude and decided to exploit him in order to rid the ancient world of all manner of dangerous, fantastical creatures. Most probably, he also counted on Heracles' demise somewhere along the way. But Heracles, crushed by tragedy and humbled by grief, was more than happy to accept the conditions.

And thus, the famous Twelve Labors of Heracles began. Initially, Eurystheus only ordered the hero to complete 10 labors—but as you'll see, the king would later be slow to keep his word.

Twelve Labors of Heracles

First:NemeanLion

The Nemean lion wasn't just any dangerous beast; it had been raised by Hera and was the offspring of a chimera, a monstrous half-snake, half-woman. Its fur was impervious to blows. This property was soon discovered by Heracles when he finally found the beast andt riedt oshoot it with arrows.

The hero realized he had no way of killing the lion other than with his bare hands. So he lured it back into its cave, where he stunned it with a blow of a club, and then strangled it to death—much as he had done with the vicioussnake sw hen he was still a baby.

Even after the lion's death, its skin was impossible to get off its body. Heracles was finally advised by Athena to use one of the beast's own claws to cut the skin. He did, and he made a cloak from the skin, which, along with his mighty club, became a part of his signature attire.

When Heracles came back to Argos and presented his trophy to Eurystheus, the king shivered with fear; he was terrified even of the sight of the skin taken off the Nemean lion's back. He forbade Heracles from entering the city ever again. From now on, he was to display the proof of his exploits outside the city gates, and his message was to be taken by a herald to the king. And thus, Eurystheus gave the evidence of his cowardice.

Second:LernaeanHydra

Slaying the Lernaean hydra was a personal revenge for Heracles. The monster had been raised by Hera for the sole purpose of killing our hero. It lived in water, had multiple snake-like heads, and whenever one head was cut off, two would grow in its place. What was more, the hydra's blood was so poisonous that even its scent could be deadly. Heracles was up for an uneasy task.

As he approached the swampy Lake Lerna, the hydra's abode, Heracles covered his mouth and nose with a cloth to protect himself from poisonous vapors. He tried shooting at the monster with his arrows, but it was, yet again, invulnerable. The task seemed impossible given the hydra's extraordinary powers of regeneration and the fact that once the monster had at least one head still alive, it was unconquerable.

So Heracles devised a plan. The ancient author Apollodorus credits the hero's nephew—and according to some (Plutarch et al., 1683/1992), also lover, Iolaus, with its design. Every time the hero cut off one of the heads, the neck wound had to be immediately cauterized with fire so that the heads wouldn't grow back (Apollodorus & Hard, 1921/1998). Iolaus then took on the task of cauterizing, while Heracles was cutting off the heads. But even then, Hera sent a giant crab to distract the hero—luckily, he crushed it with his foot.

The last head of the hydra was cut off using a magical sword gifted to Heracles by Athena. Then, it was buried as a sacrifice, and after the deed was done, Heracles dipped his arrows in the hydra's poisonous blood so that they would kill anyone they even touched.

The task was complete, and Heracles returned to Argos. But when Eurystheus learned that Iolaus helped the hero, he announced that the deed didn't count toward the number of 10 labors and sent Heracles away to complete another task.

Three:CeryneianHind

Eurystheus wasn't happy with Heracles' success to date. So the third labor was of a different kind: The hero was supposed to capture the Ceryneian hind (deer) that was so fast it could outrun arrows. Because of that, it was practically impossible to spot. It was also a sacred animal of the goddess of the hunt, Artemis, and so, by ascribing this task to Heracles, Eurystheus hoped the hero would enrage the goddess.

It took Heracles months to find the deer. Finally, one night he was able to spot it because of the way the moonlight reflected on its antlers as it ran. Heracles set on a mad hunt: It took him a full year of running after the animal to finally capture it in its sleep.

But when Heracles was carrying the hind, he encountered Artemis, as well as her brother Apollo, in the woods. He fell to his knees and begged the goddess for forgiveness. He explained the terms of his agreement with Eurystheus and the task the king had given him. He also promised to return the hind to its natural environment as soon as it was presented to the king,e ven if it went against Eurystheus' wishes.

Artemis, moved by the hero's plight, forgave him. She promised Heracles she would help him in returning the hind to the woods. Unsurprisingly, the moment Eurystheus saw the hind, he declared that it was now to be a part of the royal menagerie.

"That is all well," Heracles said, "but I have only one condition. The king must come and take the deer from me himself."

Emboldened by his recent success, Eurystheus battled his fear and came down to the city gates. Heracles made a gesture as if he was handing over the reins of the hind to the king—but the moment he let them go, the swift animalse t out to a run and was gone in a flash.

"You were simply not fast enough, my king," Heracles commented, and Eurystheus retreated to the city in rage and shame. He needed to devise a revenge plan: The next task must be especially dangerous.

Four: Erymanthian Boar

The Erymanthian boar was enormous and completely untamed. Yet again, the task was not to kill it but to bring it to Eurystheus alive. Heracles didn't know how to do it. He needed advice, so he decided to go to the centaurs.

Half-men, half-horses, the centaurs were Heracles' old friends. They lived in caves in the mountains and were wise beyond human knowledge. When Heracles came to the cave of his close friend Pholus, the centaurs advised him to chase the boar into thick snow where it would become exhausted and easier to trap. Grateful for the advice, Heracles shared a jug of wine with the two centaurs and their many friends.

But the centaurs, despite being wise, had no experience with human wine, and they didn't know that they had to dilute it with water. Too quickly, they became drunk and rowdy, and they started attacking Heracles. In self-defense, the hero had to shoot many of them with his poisonousarrow s.

And then, tragedy occurred. Pholus, who was also drunk, picked up one of Heracles' arrows, amazed at how the weapon managed to kill so many centaurs. However, his hand was shaking, and the poison from the flint dripped onto his hoof. He died in agony, and Heracles lamented over him.

But the labor still needed to be completed. So Heracles took the centaurs' advice and chased the Erymanthian boar until he exhausted it and trapped it in snow, binding it in chains. When he brought it back to Eurystheus, the king was so terrified that he hid in a pithos—a large container jar—and refused to come out until Heracles got rid of the beast. The hero did so, but nothingc oulde rase the humiliation of the king.

Unless, that is, he ascribed another labor to Heracles and one that was supposed to be both impossible and humiliating.

Five:AugeanStables

King Augeas was known for his legendary messiness. His stables were especially unkempt since he had been tasked with housing divine, immortal cattle who produced impossible amounts of dung. For Heracles to be tasked with cleaning after them was a humiliation, speaking nothing of the impossibility. Nobody dared to clean the stables for 30 years.

Heracles struck a deal with Augeas: If he managed to clean the stables in a day, he would receive one-tenth of the cattle. Augeas agreed readily since the task seemed impossibleany way.

But Heracles had a plan. Near the stables, two rivers, Alpheus and Peneus, were running their courses. With his supernatural strength, Heracles upended some boulders and diverted the course of the rivers, running them right through the stables and cleaning them of all the filth.

Augeas was very happy with the service, but he refused to give Heracles his reward. He reasoned that the hero had been employed to perform the task by Eurystheus anyway, and it made their agreement void. Heracles tried to argue his case in court, but when it failed, he killed Augeas in a rage and gave the kingdom to Augeas'son.

When Heracles returned to Argos with his reward, Eurystheus, yet again, decreed that this labor was not to be counted among the number ascribed to our hero. The river did all the work, the king reasoned, and anyway, Heracles was paid for his trouble. Soon, Eurystheus would have a new task for Heracles to perform.

Six:StymphalianBirds

Yet again, Heracles was tasked with defeating monsters. The Stymphalian birds were the sacred birds of Ares, the violent god of war. They ate manflesh and had beaks made of bronze that could shred their victims to pieces; their dung was poisonous, too. They lived near Lake Stymphalia in northeastern Greece, where they destroyed the local crops and terrorized the populace.

Heracles needed to scare the birds out of their abode in order to kill them. For this, the goddess Athena gave him a special rattle. It worked like magic: The birds flew into the sky, scared, and Heracles killed many of them with his poisoned arrows. The rest were so terrified that they flew away, never to return to the area.

Seven:CretanBull

Eurystheus, still dissatisfied with Heracles' imperviousness, this time sent him on a task that would take him far from the Greek mainland to the island of Crete. The Cretan bull was the father of the famous monster Minotaur, born of the monstrous union between that bull and Queen Pasiphaë, who had been cursed to fall in love with him by the god of the sea, Poseidon, after a sacrifice gone wrong.

Heracles was tasked to capture the bull and bring it back to Argos. When he related his task to King Minos of Crete, the monarch offered his help. But Heracles declined: If he were to be aided, Eurystheus might dismiss the labor again. So yet again, Heracles used the extraordinary power of his muscles, sneaking up on the bull from behind and throttling it just enough to make it pliant.

It was of no surprise to anyone that when Heracles came back with the bull, Eurystheus hid in his pithos jar at the mere sight of the creature. He then ordered it to be sacrificed to Hera, but since the goddess still hated Heracles and the sacrifice would be a proof of his glory, she rejected it. The bull was released and would later wreak havoc around the area of Maraton.

Eight:MaresofDiomedes

Diomedes was a king of the island of Thrace and a demigod himself: He was a son of Ares. In keeping with the violent, unpredictable nature of his father, he kept man-eating horses in his stables. They breathed fire and ate anyone who trespassed on the land. Diomedes was a tyrant, and his mares were the instrument of his tyranny.

Heracles' task was to steal the horses. The hero is said to have come to the island with a number of companions, among whom was Abderus, another one of his lovers. The boy helped Heracles to cut the chains while Diomedes was distracted and was tasked with keeping the horses in check while the hero went to fight the tyrant king.

Tragically, Heracles didn't know about the horses' man-eating abilities, and when he came back with an overpowered Diomedes in tow, he found Abderus' bloody and half-eaten corpse. In a rage, Heracles fed Diomedes to his own horses. Then, he founded the city of Abdera on the island of Thrace in honor of his late companion.

The horses, when they were full and sated by the human flesh, became more pliant. This allowed Heracles to bind their mouths and lead them back to Argos. There are conflicting versions as to what happened to them afterwards: Some say that they were sacrificed to Hera (Rose, 2013), others, to Zeus (who refused the sacrifice and sent wild beasts to kill them), and yet others that they became perpetually calm and were allowed to roam the fields of Argos freely (Leeming, 1998). However it happened, the eighth labor was complete.

Nine:BeltofHippolyta

The Ninth Labor of Heracles is the one that brings us to a meeting with another demigod whose story I'm about to tell in this chapter. Hippolyta was queen of the Amazons, a legendary warlike tribe of women. I will talk about her more in the latter part of this chapter; now,w e'll only focus on Heracles' task.

Hippolyta's belt was known for its extraordinary properties, as it was a war belt given to her by her divine father, Ares. Eurystheus wished Heracles to retrieve it since his daughter Admete craved it greatly. The hero set off on a long and difficult journey: The land of the Amazons lay very far away in the east. He took a bunch of friends and companions, and on the way, they fought several battles with various aggressors.

When they finally reached the Amazonian land of Themiscyra, Heracles decided to complete his task in a civil manner. He called for an audience with the queen, and she, impressed with his exploits, agreed to give him the belt willingly.

But Hera was still intent on destroying our hero. When Hippolyta entered Heracles' ship in order to complete the gift giving, Hera disguised herself as one of the Amazons and started creating rumors that Heracles intended to capture and kidnap the queen. The Amazons were in turmoil and rode out to confront the hero. He, in turn, thought that it was Hippolyta who had planned a treacherous ambush, so, as a result of a tragic misunderstanding, he killed her and fled to Argos, taking the belt with him.

Ten: Cattle of Geryon

Geryon was a giant with three heads. He lived on the island of Erytheia with his cattle. The livestock itself didn't seem to have any supernatural properties; it was their guardian that was more fearsome. But still, even though Heracles' journey to the island located in the far west of the Greek world was a long one, he managed to kill Geryon relatively quickly with his poisoned arrows.

Transporting the cattle back to Argos was no simple task. Hera tried to thwart Heracles yet again, sending flies that annoyed the cattle that were dispersed over a large terrain. It took the hero over a year to collect them again. In later, Roman versions of the myth, Heracles traveled with the cattle over the Aventine Hill, which would later become the site of Rome (Eusebius, 1818/2008). There, he was supposed to have been thwarted by a giant named Cacus, who stole some of his cattle. Heracles killed him and built an altar in a place that would later become the Roman cattle market.

Eleven: Golden Apples of the Hesperides

Now came the time of the two additional labors that Eurystheus ascribed to Heracles, claiming that the slaying of the hydra and cleaning of the Augean stables didn't count. The king wanted the last two tasks to be especially difficult—and so, he ordered him to steal the apples fromt he Garden of the Hesperides themselves.

The Hesperides were the nymphs, minor nature goddesses in ancient Greek mythology. Their task was to guard the golden evening light of the sunset—no wonder the apples from their garden were of the legendary golden color.

There was only one problem—no mortal knew where the Garden of the Hesperides was located. They were living somewhere in the far west, where the sun set every day, and probably very close to the edge of the world, since they were daughters of the Titan Atlas, who carried the whole world on his shoulders. So Heracles' first task was to learn of the location of the garden.

The knowledge was imparted to him by the Old Man of the Sea, a primordial sea god whom Heracles captured. The hero's journey was to be long and arduous, and it led through Egypt, where he was almost sacrificed but burstfromhisc hains.

Finally, Heracles arrived at the garden and was immediately confronted by Atlas, who stood there holding the world on his shoulders. Heracles devised a plan: He asked Atlas to go to the garden and retrieve the apples from his daughters while he, with the extraordinary power of his muscles, would hold the Earth for a little while. Atlas, weary with his task, readily agreed.

When the Titan came back, he wasn't willing to swap places with Heracles again. Finally, he felt light and free, and he didn't want to give that up. Heracles had to be clever if he was to leave his spot ever again.

"I can hold the world for the rest of time," he said, "as long as you keep it for just a moment longer. I need to adjustmy cloak."

Atlas, who was perhaps the strongest, but not the brightest of beings, agreed. As soon as the weight of the world left Heracles' shoulders, he made for his escape, taking the golden apples with him.

In Argos, Heracles was met with Eurystheus' fury. The king had thought that he had already seen the last of the hero: The task that he had set upon him had seemed impossible. And yet, here he was, having brought the apples.

It was the time for the last labor.

Twelve:Cerberus

This was supposed to be the crown of all previous tasks: Cerberus, the mighty, bloodthirsty, three-headed dog that guarded the gate to Hades, the ancient Greek Underworld. Capturing him and bringing him to the light seemed completely impossible. So, that was precisely what Eurystheus ordered Heracles to do.

To enter the Underworld, Heracles had to undergo a special ritual of initiation and purification: the Eleusinian Mysteries. Then, two gods, Athena and Hermes, became his guides to the world of the dead.

The task was accomplished splendidly. Heracles didn't use any weapons to overpower Cerberus. Instead, he caught him with his bare hands and flung him over his back. Unsurprisingly, King Eurystheus, who had been scared of a boar and a bull before, was absolutely terrified of the infernal dog and hid in his pithos yet again. He was, in fact, so scared that he begged Heracles to bring Cerberus back to the Underworld and promisedt ore lease him from his slavery at last.

Thus, Heracles' penance and servitude were finally over.

Other Adventures

Now that Heracles was done with his labors, he could roam the world freely in search of further adventures and glory. The exploits he would take part in at this point in his life would never become as famous as the Twelve Labors, though.

Many of Heracles' adventures included women (and, to some extent, also men). It is said that straight after he completed his Twelve Labors, he fell in love with Princess Iole from Oechalia in Thessaly. Iole's father decreed that he would give his daughter's hand in marriage to anyone who would win an archery contest. Naturally, Heracles won, but the king went back on his promise—he had been an expert archer himself and couldn't bear the humiliation. Moreover, he had heard of what happened to Megara and of Hera's hatred for Heracles, and he was afraid his daughter would meet the same end.

Iole's brother Iphitos, fearing Heracles' wrath, urged his father to reconsider his decision. But the king was adamant, and, unsurprisingly, his obstinance sent Heracles into a rage. He attacked Oechalia and killed everyone apart from Iphitos, who would later become his best friend, and Iole, whom he took as a concubine by force.

But Hera was by far not done with tormenting Heracles. Yet again, she sent a fit of madness on him, which caused him to hurl Iphitos against the city walls and kill him. For this, the hero would have to serve another penance: being a slave in the court of Queen Omphaleof Ly dia.

The story of Omphale is a fantastical tale whose sources lie in Greek misogyny and ideas of what a woman's role in society was. Omphale wasn't an Amazon, but she was a strong queen. She would force Heracles to do "women's work" (spinning) and wear women's clothing for a year. It's possible that through Omphale, who was supposed to be a Middle Eastern queen, the Greeks wanted to show the exoticism of the foreigners' habits. For Heracles as a Greek, this servitude was supposed to be especially shameful (Lucian of Samosata et al., 1905/2015).

Deianira and Death

In the end, it wouldn't be Hera's revenge but Heracles' own decisions that would contribute to his demise. His death would be caused indirectly by his lack of restraint in relations with women. Because while still trying to win Iole, right before he came back to Oechalia to destroy it, Heracles met Deianira and, forgetting about

Iole for a while, won her from the river god Achelous andmarrie dhe r.

But soon after Heracles married Deianira, he went back to Iole and won her as well. Deianira didn't like that turn of events and was afraid that Heracles would stop lovinghe rsinc e Iole was very beautiful.

One day, Deianira and Heracles were traveling through the river Evinos in western Greece. The river was deep and turbulent, and there was no boat or bridge. But a wild centaur by the name of Nessus guarded the passage and would sometimes agree to transport the travelers on his back. Crossing the river was not a problem for Heracles, but Deianira decided to use the centaur's services.

While Deianira was on his back, Nessus attempted to rape her. When Heracles realized what was happening, he shot the centaur with one of his poisoned arrows and rescued his wife. But as he was dying, Nessus whispered far more poisonous words into Deianira's ear: Her husband might have rescued her from a centaur, but he surely didn't love her anymore. After all, he was *Heracles*—he had a new concubine and had fathered illegitimate children all across Greece. But if Deianira took a sample of Nessus' blood and mixed it with olive oil, she could create a magical potion that would ensure Heracles would never be unfaithful again.

Deianira's insecurity made her listen to the centaur's words. She took the sample and created the potion, but she didn't use it for a while, instead saving it. She still tried to win Heracles' affection by traditional means, but after it became clear that the hero's love for Iole was only growing, she decided to take action.

So she took Heracles' signature skin of the Nemean lion and smeared it with the potion. In an ironic, cruel way, Nessus hadn't been lying. The potion really ensured that Heracles would never be unfaithful again... because he would die. It was Nessus' revenge frombe yond the grave.

When Heracles put on the garment, his skin started burning terribly. It was the poison of the hydra mixed with Nessus' poisonous blood. The pain was unbearable. The hero still couldn't die, but he couldn't live either—so he built a funeral pyre for himself and begged anyone to light it. Nobody would do it except for Heracles' companion and lover, Iolaus and Philoctetes, a Greek hero who would later inherit Heracles' bow and arrows and become a famous archer int he Trojan War.

Deianira, distraught by what she had unwittingly done, committed suicide.

But Heracles' story wasn't over with his death. His mortal body burned, but the immortal part of his soul returned to Zeus and became immediately admitted amongt he gods in Olympus as a demigod fully deified.

Heracles' story is a fascinating tale of adventure, love, and tragedy. In a way, the catalog of his labors serves as a guide to the supernatural menagerie of Greek mythology. He's the epitome of a hero and an archetype for many heroic figures in the tradition of the

Greeks, the Romans, and later, of many other Europeannat ions.

The Story of Hippolyta

I have already mentioned Hippolyta insofar as her tragic death coincided with one of Heracles' labors. But her figure transcends her dalliance with this famous hero, proving that even in the fairly misogynistic Greek culture, there was some space for strong female characters.

Hippolyta was a demigod through her father, the god of war Ares. Her mother, Otrera, was the first Amazon and the founder of the Amazon kingdom. The Amazons in Greek writings are a classic example of "othering"—writing about a fantastical society in which the usual social norms were inverted, providing the reader with both a sense of fascination and fear. Thus, the Amazons were warrior women who surpassed men in activities such as archery, hunting, riding, and combat, and their kingdom was exclusively feminine. If a boy was born, they would either expose him to death or give him away for fostering and would only interact with men briefly in order to reproduce.

The Amazons are said to have taken part in a number of conflicts throughout Greek history, mythological and historical, one of them being the Trojan War. Their engagement in warfare would always mean an enormous advantage to whatever side they were fightingon.

But let us come back to Hippolyta. She had two sisters, Antiope and Melanippe, and she wore her famous belt, which had been a gift from her father, Ares. We got the first glimpse of her story when she encountered Theseus, a fully human, but very famous Greek hero. Theseus is said to have abducted her—some said, with the help of Heracles himself. The abduction of the queen of the Amazons was supposed to serve as an elevation of Theseus' prowess.

The accounts of what happened afterward vary. Theseus was supposed to have taken Hippolyta to his home, Athens, and the Amazons, enraged by the insult of their queen's abduction, rallied and attacked the city, instigating a conflict that would later be known as the Attic War. During the battle, Hippolyta was supposed to have been killed by accident by an Amazon named Molpadia.

But another account claims that Hippolyta went willingly with Theseus, and the war was caused by the fact that he later set her aside for another woman, Phaedra (Graves, 2017). Or, yet another story says that no war took place, and Hippolyta lived with Theseus for a number of years and bore him a son, Hippolytus of Athens. In this version, she later died in the tragic encounter with Heracles, which I have already described (Graves, 2017). In reality, the stories of Hippolyta might be a conflation of tales about several different women—possibly some of them being her sisters.

Hippolyta, even if the tales about her are fragmentary, is a fascinating figure. Her existence outside of the Greek gender norms gives her a special status, despite the tellers of her tales always taking special pains to depict male heroes as being the ones to subdue her. Her character, as well as the nature of the Amazons, have inspired storytellers from Shakespeare to Rick Riordan and have become an ideal to strive for to all women who devote their lives to athleticism or military service.

Helen of Sparta

Another famous woman demigod, probably more famous than Hippolyta, is, at the same time, completely different from her. Where Hippolyta was known for her military prowess, Helen's main attribute was her otherworldly beauty. This would, more often than not, makehe rapaw nint he games of powerful men.

Helen's Birth and Childhood

But let us start from the beginning. Helen's mother, Leda, was a princess who became the queen of Sparta. Zeus admired her beauty and wished to seduce her— which he did, disguised as a swan. Playing a victim, he flew into Leda's arms, seemingly seeking protection from an eagle. But the moment he found himself in her lap, an unusual union took place. On the same night, Leda had intercourse with her human husband, Tyndareus. As a result of these pairings, two eggs were hatched in her body: one containing Helen and her sister Clytemnestra and the other containing male twins Castor and Pollux. The ancient authors would never be entirely sure which of the children were human and which were demigods (Apollodorus & Hard, 1921/1998; Pepin, 2008)—but the most common version is that from each egg, one child only was the offspring of Zeus: Helen and Pollux were half-divine, while Clytemnestra and Castor were human (Euripides &Allan,1891/2013) .

Castor and Pollux would later become a famous duo known as the Dioscuri, an example of a brotherly love that transcended immortality. But their role in Helen's story would be no less important.

Right from her girlhood, Helen was exceptionally beautiful—and it attracted men. When Helen was only 7, Theseus, that well-known abductor of women, vowed to his friend Pirithous that they both should obtain divine wives and daughters of Zeus. So, Pirithous was supposed to help him abduct Helen, while Theseus would help him with his pursuit of Persephone.

Theseus stole Helen right from under her mother's nose and then left her with his mother, Aethra, presumably to wait until she became of marriageable age. Castor and Pollux, even though they were still boys, couldn't abide by what happened. They invaded Theseus' city, Athens, while the hero was away in Hades and captured it, instating their own puppet king in Theseus' place and taking Helen with Aethra back to Sparta. There they forced Aethra to become Helen's slave. She would only be returned to Athens years later after the Trojan War.

The incident with Theseus, if anything, was a sign of the things to come. Soon, when Helen became of age, swarms of suitors started coming to Sparta and begging for her hand. But it was fraught with danger. Her human foster-father, King Tyndareus, knew that whoever would win his favor would inevitably become the enemy of everyone else and a war might start over Helen's hand.

It was Odysseus who proposed a solution. He went to Sparta more with an intent to observe the proceedings than to win Helen: He knew that as king of a small island, Ithaca, he had little chance of winning. So he came up with an oath. Every suitor should swear that no matter who won Helen's hand, they would protect the winner and swear not to harm him; even more, they would swear to come to his aid in case of any danger or transgression. It was a clever solution at the time— everyone counted on his victory, and so everyone wanted to be protected. The oath was agreed upon by Tyndareus and sworn readily by all the suitors.

Little did Odysseus know that it would be precisely this oatht hat would later trigger the Trojan War.

The Second Abduction

Helen was won by Menelaus, who later became the king of Sparta. We are not told whether Helen was happy with that choice or not, but in any case, for about 10 years, all seemed well.

Thatis,unt ilP arisc ame to Sparta.

Paris, a Trojan prince, had gotten himself entangled in a very supernatural affair. During the wedding of Peleus and Thetis—the parents of yet another famous demigod, Achilles—a blunder was made. Even though all the gods and goddesses had been invited for the celebration, the goddess of discord, Eris, had been excluded—nobody wanted discord during their wedding party. But she came anyway and decided to wreak havoc among the guests.

Eris came with a golden apple. The inscription on the apple said that it was intended for the most beautiful goddess. And since the Greek goddesses weren't exactly known for their maturity and restraint, immediately three of them claimed that the apple had been clearly intended for them: Hera, Athena, and Aphrodite. A judgment had to be pronounced, preferably by an outsider.

The god Hermes led the three warring goddesses to Paris. The young man had been his choice because not only was he humble—even though a prince, he occupied himself with herding sheep—but he had judged justly before, awarding a prize in a bull contest to Ares even though his own bull had competed as well. Hermes found Paris on the slopes of Mount Ida and presented the problem to him.

But it seemed that this time, the judgment would prove too much for Paris. All the goddesses looked to him beautiful beyond imagining; after all, they were *goddesses*. What was more, all of them immediately started trying to win him over by proposing favors. Hera promised to make Paris the king of Europe and Asia combined; Athena offered wisdom; but it was the gift of Aphrodite that made Paris crack in the end. She promised him Helen, the most beautiful woman in the world.

And so, Aphrodite won the contest, and Paris was ready to take the opportunity and abduct Helen to Troy.

He claimed to have come to Sparta under the guise of a diplomatic mission. The ancient sources are contradictory on what exactly transpired between him and Helen. Some authors say that he raped and abducted her (Herodotus, 1849/2015), while others say she was unhappy with Menelaus and went willingly (Sappho & Chandler, 1733/1998).

However it happened, this incident would cause the greatest conflict in the legendary history of ancient Greece: the Trojan War. All the kings and princes of Greece, bound by their oath to protect the husband of Helen, were now called to arms by Menelaus. Troops started assembling. Soon, they would sail to Troy.

The Trojan War

Becoming Paris' consort, Helen was initially welcomed into the Trojan society. But as the war waged on for years, becoming more and more destructive for both sides, the Trojans began to shun and hate Helen. Apart from Paris, only her new father-in-law, King Priam, and her brother-in-law, Hector, were kind to her. And as the time passed, Helen also started seeing Paris' shortcomings: He wasn't quick to protect her, and he was rather cowardly when it came to battle. It was

Hector who commanded the defense of the city; Hector who would take on challenges of great Greek warriors, including Achilles himself. In the *Iliad*, there is a hint of Helen growing quite attached to Hector, and shunningP aris(Homere t al., 1924/2003).

But Hector was finally killed by Achilles, who was seeking revenge for the death of his companion, Patroclus. Helen remained in Troy with nearly no allies. Soon, Paris himself would also be mortally wounded by the Greek Philoctetes and would die from his wounds.

Now, Helen truly became like an object to be disposed of. After a short debate about which one of Paris' younger brothers should marry Helen after his death, the lot fell to Deiphobus, whom Helen didn't love.

Ultimately, the Trojan War ended when Odysseus came up with his signature idea of creating the Trojan horse: a supposed gift of the Greeks to the Trojans which, nonetheless, contained armed Greek warriors who swarmed the city after sunset. According to Homer, Helen knew about—or, at least, suspected—the ruse, and she came up to the horse, imitating the cries of women whom the Greeks left behind, trying to dishearten them (Homer et al., 1924/2010). It's not entirely sure what Helen's goal was in this; it's possible that it was a scene included solely to further tarnish Helen's character.

During the fall of Troy, it is said that Helen hid her new husband's sword to get rid of him. Otherwise, the accounts of her behavior during the carnage are contradictory. Some depict her as cruelly rejoicing in the fall of the Trojans but others as lost and alone, wandering the streets of the city and crying (Suzuki, 1992).

At last, Helen was confronted by her Spartan husband, Menelaus. Seeing the figure of a person who, in his eyes, had brought 10 years of bloody war upon the Greeks, he raised his sword to kill her. But at that moment, Helen unveiled herself, and seeing her unfaltering beauty, Menelaus dropped his sword.

After the War

It is said that after the Greek forces returned home, Helen lived peacefully with Menelaus for a number of years again. But one day, she went away to the island of Rhodes where her good former friend Polyxo lived. However, Polyxo had lost her husband in the Trojan War and was now set on getting her revenge. She invited Helen to live with her under false pretenses and then captured her and hanged her from a tree. Another account has Thetis, Achilles' mother, sacrificing Helen to the gods as a punishment for her son's death (Grimal, 2000).

Helen is a very ambiguous figure. As I hope you could see throughout her story, the sources were fundamentally conflicted on her responsibility for the war. Some authors depicted her as a cruel traitor, others as a tragic woman. Her inherited divine beauty was definitely more of a curse than a blessing. Many Greek demigods shared a tragic fate, caught between humanity and divinity—but for Helen, the fate seemed to have been especially cruel.

The Story of Achilles

Achilles closes our selection of Greek demigods. Even though he is probably just as well-known as Heracles, it's nonetheless not as widely recognized that he was a demigod, too.

Unusually, Achilles wasn't a son of Zeus or other male god of the Greek pantheon, but of Thetis, a sea nymph, or a goddess of water, and Peleus, a mortal man. An interesting story is tied to this union: Zeus was interested in pursuing Thetis, but he heard a prophecy spoken by the Titan Prometheus. It said that the goddess was destined to give birth to a son who would surpass his father. The king of gods, who had already deposed his father to take the rule of Olympus, had been perpetually afraid of the same fate meeting him, so he quickly arranged a marriage for Thetis to a mortal.

Achilles' Childhood

Peleus was the king of the Myrmidons in Phthia, and his marriage to Thetis was turbulent from the start— even their wedding was marred by the famous Judgment of Paris. Before Achilles was born, the wheels of fate that would eventually bring his demise were turned into motion.

It is said that when Achilles was a baby, Thetis wanted to make him semi-immortal by being impervious to all blows. So she either bathed him in the river Styx (the river dividing the world of the living from the

Underworld), or she anointed him with ambrosia and then tried to burn away his mortality in fire.

But while she was doing this, suddenly, Peleus entered the room. Terrified at his wife apparently burning their son in the fireplace, he leaped at her and stopped her. Enraged, Thetis scorned him for being a foolish man who couldn't understand the ways of the gods. Then, she left in fury, never to be seen by her husband again. The process of making Achilles' skin impenetrable was incomplete: Thetis had been holding him by his heel, so from now on, this would become the only part of his body that would be vulnerable to blows—the famous Achilles'he el.

But before she left, Thetis spoke a prophecy. Achilles' fate could be twofold: Either he lived a long and happy life in complete obscurity or his life would be short and tragic but full of heroic deeds and his name would be known for all posterity. It's probably easy to surmise which fate came into fruition in the end.

When Achilles was a boy, his father gave him away to the wise centaur Chiron for fostering. We have already met Chiron briefly during Heracles' tragic encounter with the centaurs. Chiron was skilled in all manner of arts: medicine, herbs, music, archery, gymnastics, and prophecy. He was a perfect tutor for a perfect hero.

Around the same time, Achilles met Patroclus. The boy had been sent to Peleus for fostering after he had killed a child in anger over some game. Achilles' presence had a tempering effect on Patroclus since they soon became fast friends. The early sources, such as Homer, don't mention explicitly that Achilles and Patroclus' relationship was anything more than friendship; however, many later authors interpreted their bond as that of lovers (Morales & Mariscal, 2003).

Hidden From the War

That Thetis had left Peleus didn't mean that she had no contact with her son or that she didn't try to influence his fate. When the first news came about the Greek troops gathering for the Trojan War, she hid Achilles in the court of Lycomedes, king of Skyros. Achilles was disguised as a girl, which was not a difficult task given his extraordinary beauty. There, he had a short dalliance with the king's daughter, Deidamia, with whom he had two sons.

But the search for Achilles was relentless. Odysseus, that clever hero, had learned from an oracle that the Greeks would be unable to capture Troy without Achilles, so he searched for him in every corner of Greece.

At last, he came to Skyros. Odysseus disguised himself as a traveling salesman selling trinkets and various goods and put a veritable display before Lycomedes' daughters: earrings and necklaces, bracelets and rings. But there was also a spear among the goods. When a redheaded girl called Pyrrha came over to Odysseus' stand, she immediately picked up the spear. Odysseus caught her hand and unveiled her—this was Achilles.

Achilles wasn't forced to come to the war. He was convinced by Odysseus and came willingly, craving a lifefullofglory —to his mother's chagrin.

The Sail to Troy

And so, Achilles, along with Patroclus, sailed to Aulis, where all the Greek troops gathered before their collective journey to Troy. But there was one problem: no wind. Apparently, one of the Greek kings, the famous Agamemnon, had hunted and killed a deer in a sacred grove dedicated to Artemis, so the goddess of hunt punished the fleet. Stranded at Aulis, the Greeks grew discontented and angry. At last, a seer told Agamemnon terrible news. There was only one way to appeaseArt emis—to sacrifice his daughter, Iphigenia.

So Agamemnon, torn between his duty and his familial love, wrote to his wife, Clytemnestra, to come to Aulis and bring Iphigenia with her. He gave a false reason, saying Iphigenia was to be married to Achilles before the Greeks sailed for the war.

Achilles himself had no idea what Agamemnon's real plan was. In fact, he wasn't even aware of the ruse. He learned the news of his apparent "marriage" during an accidental conversation with Clytemnestra when the women had already arrived at Aulis. From word to word, they both arrived at a terrible conclusion—there was no marriage to be held; Agamemnon had other, terrible plans. And so, Achilles, enraged on behalf of Iphigenia (and fearing for unwittingly participating in a dishonorable deed), confronted Agamemnon. He vowed that he would do everything in his power to prevent Iphigenia's death.

But the Greek troops were turning rowdy and turbulent. Somehow, the rumor about the only solution to their plight got out, so people were now besieging Agamemnon's tent. Now there was the danger that if Achilles didn't comply with their wishes, they would shredt opie ces both Agamemnon and him.

Hearing all this, Iphigenia made her own decision. She decided to sacrifice herself for the greater good of the Greeks and went to her death resigned and unafraid. Achilles, who had been prepared to defend Iphigenia bodily,w asinimme nseaw e of her courage.

The whole incident is described in Euripides' play *Iphigenia in Aulis*. The play ends with the messenger coming to Clytemnestra and telling her that in the last moment, the merciful gods had replaced Iphigenia's body with that of a deer and whisked her away. This, however, is widely considered to be a later addition (Euripides et al., 1891/2004). The original text has the inevitability of a cruel tragedy and our hero, Achilles, admiringt he courage of a woman.

During the War

Homer's *Iliad* starts with the words on Achilles' wrath—probably the most famous lines from this epic poem: "The wrath do thou sing, O goddess, of Peleus' son, Achilles…" (Homer et al., 1924/2003). But what caused it and why did it become such a central theme in the story of the Trojan War?

The *Iliad* starts in the middle of the war—in fact, years after the Greeks had come to the Trojan shores. They had been unable to capture the city, and now, King Agamemnon had insulted the god Apollo by enslaving Chryseis, a Trojan woman who was the daughter of Apollo's priest. The god had sent a plague among the Greeks for that, and the prophet Calchas—the same who decreed that Iphigenia had to be sacrificed for the favorable wind—pointed out the reason for the misfortune in Achilles' presence. He agreed to speak of this to Agamemnon but only if Achilles vowed to protect him from the king's anger.

Achilles made a promise and went before the king with Calchas. After hearing the news, Agamemnon agreed to return Chryseis to her father, but he demanded instead to be recompensed by another slave. The choice fell on Achilles' own slave and "spoil of war," Briseis.

Achilles felt insulted by the request. He could hardly refuse his king, especially when the future of the Greek army was at stake, but not only did he feel humiliated, he was heartbroken—he had grown quite attached to Briseis.

On the same night when the exchange happened, Thetis came to her son and urged him to refuse to fight for the Greeks. Achilles did so, and in turn, he asked his mother to convince Zeus to give a temporary advantage to the Trojans so that Agamemnon might see his mistakeandAc hilles'honormight be re turned.

And so the battle for Achilles' favor started. The Greeks soon saw that the Trojans were winning and started urging Achilles to come back. Agamemnon promised him all his spoils of war, including the return of Briseis. But the hero was too far gone in his anger and refused. What was more, he started urging other Greeks to stop fighting.

Meanwhile, Hector, the heir to the throne of Troy, wrought havoc among the Greek troops. The situation began to be desperate. Without Achilles, no one could stop him, and he soon drove the Greek forces all the way to the coastline.

Seeing the destruction among the Greek forces, Patroclus, who had been occupying the tent with Achilles, decided to intervene. He donned Achilles' armor and, disguised as his companion, led Achilles' troops into battle, managing to drive the Trojans away.

Seeing who he took to be Achilles, Hector readily engaged in battle with him. Patroclus, despite having learned the craft of war from Achilles himself, lacked Achilles' skill—Hector killed him.

This was the last straw for Achilles. When news came of Patroclus' deeds and death, he tore his clothes and grieved, and Thetis came to comfort him. Soon though, grief turned into rage as Achilles vowed to avenge his friend'sde ath.

Thetis convinced the god of smithcraft, Hephaestus, to make a new armor for Achilles; the one that he had been wearing had been damaged when Patroclus was killed. The armor was not only sturdy but beautiful, depicting many mythological themes, described in detail inHome r's *Iliad*.

Then, Achilles took to the field. He sought out Hector, killing innumerable men in the process. So many that the river Scamander, which encompassed Troy, was blocked by the bodies, and the god of the river issued a challenge to Achilles and battled with him.

At last, Achilles found Hector. Their duel was a long one and was observed both by the Greeks from the field and by the Trojans from the ramparts. Initially, Hector ran from Achilles, encircling the walls of Troy three times in hopes of tiring the hero—until at last Athena herself, disguised as Hector's brother Deiphobus, told him that it wasn't becoming of him to postpone the fight further. Hector realized that the battle was now inevitable—and had a sinking feeling that he was going to die.

When it became clear that Hector was losing—he thrust his spear at Achilles but missed—he begged the Greek hero to treat his body with dignity after he died. In response, Achilles snarled that he could give no such guarantee; Hector had killed his beloved friend and his rage was now beyond measuring.

And Achilles kept his word. He killed Hector and dragged his body in dirt behind his chariot around the walls of Troy—to the great chagrin of all the Trojans, and especially King Priam. After he was done, he held funeralgame sinhonorofP atroclus.

During the night, King Priam himself, having donned a disguise, came to Achilles' tent. He begged the young hero to give him back his son's body so that he could at least bury him with honors. He cried and went on his knees, and at last, something cracked in the surface of Achilles' unquenchable anger. He saw an old father begging to be able to bury his beloved son. Every father should be granted such mercy and no less one whose son had been honorable. Achilles finally recognized not only Hector's honor but also the tragedy of their respective situations: Both of them had been defending what was theirs, and it was hardly Hector's fault that he had been fighting with the Greeks who were besieging his city. At last, Achilles relented and gave Priam Hector's body. For nine days, there was to be a truce between the Greeks and the Trojans so that Priam could hold the funerary ceremonies in peace.

Achilles' Death

The *Iliad* doesn't describe what happened in the war after Hector's death. But from other accounts (Quintus de Smyrne & Hopkinson, 1891/2018; Abrantes, 2016) we know about Achilles' later deeds and eventual death int he Trojan War.

After the engagement with Hector, our hero fought Penthesilea, the princess of the Amazons and the sister of Hippolyta. The Amazons had been fighting on the side of the Trojans, and it was their hope that the fierce warrior woman would finally defeat Achilles. It is said that when Achilles engaged in the battle with her, he was initially overcome by her beauty and didn't fight as much as he'd meant to, but when he realized his mistake, he redoubled his efforts and killed her. He mourned her straight afterward—not only for her beauty but also for her military prowess.

Achilles' death came very close to the Greeks' last charge into Troy, right around the time of the ruse with the Trojan horse. The effect of Peleus' tragic mistake, when he prevented Thetis from making Achilles' skin fully impenetrable, now came to fruition. Paris shot Achilles in the heel with one of his arrows, and the hero soon bled to death. As per request, Achilles' bones were mixed with those of Patroclus on his funeral pyre and enclosed together in a golden case procured by Thetis.

And that is how the hero's life came to a close: It was short, but eventful—full of glory, but most of all, passion. Achilles' wrath had no equals, but it seemed he was just as quick to love as he was to hate.

Achilles closes my selection of Greek demigods. In the next chapter, I will talk about a very different mythological tradition. We will leave the sunny Greek shores and venture into the cold northern lands of modern Scandinavia, to meet half-divine heroes from the Norse tradition.

Chapter 2:

Norse Mythology

There might be some similarities between the Norse and Greek traditions when it comes to gods and their attributes, but there is also one fundamental difference: Where Greek myths abound in demigods, the Norse ones have a sacred few. Thor might be slightly similar to Zeus in that he was the king of the heavens and controlled the thunder, but he didn't seem to have had many affairs with human women. Similarly, Odin, though one of his titles was that of an Allfather, was a parent figure in a more metaphorical, and less literal, sense.

That doesn't mean, of course, that there are no demigods in the Norse myths. In this chapter, I will relate the stories of those we know.

Bragi

Bragi's figure can be read in two ways. On one hand, he was a fully divine figure, the god of poetry and inspiration. On the other hand, many Norse skalds (poets who composed a certain type of ornate old Norse poetry, often for special occasions) went by the name of Bragi, most probably in honor of the god. So why am I including him in the number of Norse demigods?

Bragi Boddason, or, Bragi the Old, was a famous Norwegian skald in the first part of the 9th century C.E. His historicity is sometimes doubted, but one of the theories says that he might have been a real, historical figure who was deified after death due to his exceptional skill and actually gave his name to the god Bragi (Hollander, 1945). In that case, Boddason would be an example of a fully mortal figure whose talents seemed so extraordinary that a supposition was made that they must have been divine.

Let us start our story with Bragi the man. He was said to have lived in southeastern Norway and to have been a member of a prominent family from those parts. He was a court poet to three semilegendary kings: Ragnar Lodbrok, Eysteinn Beli, and Björn at Haugi. That last king was said to have been angered at Bragi's behavior one day, which forced the skald to compose a poem to ransom his own life. Some legends also say that he had encounters with trolls (Ross, 2011).

There are a few verses in one of the preserved old Norse poems that might have come from Bragi himself. They are a part of a poem called the *Ragnarsdrápa*, composed supposedly for King Ragnar Lodbrok. Much as Homer's depiction of Achilles' shield, the *Ragnarsdrápa* is a poem about a shield that the king gifted Bragi, describing many mythological scenes depicted on that piece of armor.

Not much else is known about the historical Bragi. But when it comes to mythology, the stories about the deified human become quite interesting.

Bragi the God

As a god, Bragi was the founder of all skaldic poetry, a son of Odin with a giantess named Gunnlod, and a husband of the goddess of youth, Idunn. He wore a longbe ardandposse ssedgre at wisdom.

Bragi's role as a god of poetry was to greet any newcomers entering the hall of the gods in Asgard. It was a custom in Norse culture that this role would fall to the most eloquent person in a gathering; they would also decide if a newcomer was worthy of entering or not. So when one day, Loki, the famous Norse trickster god of mischief, demanded to enter the hall, Bragi forbade him from doing so—he knew that the presence of this god could only mean trouble. But Odin overruled him, so Loki entered the hall and insulted each and every one of the gods gathered there. The exact insults are all gathered in an old Norse poem called the *Lokasenna* (Dronke, 1969). In the end, Bragi was the last one to be berated by Loki, and he was accused of cowardice since he was afraid to let him enter.

There is no continuous narrative preserved of Bragi's life, and he mostly appears on the fringes of more famous stories about the exploits of gods such as Odin orLoki.

Sigi

Sigi in himself isn't a very noteworthy figure: a demigod through the virtue of being a son of Odin. He is more of an origin story than a hero in his own right. His importance comes from a different source—he was the ancestral figure behind the clan of the Völsungs, one of the most prominent families in the old Norse and Germanic legends.

One of the few things we know about Sigi is that he was a short-tempered man. One day, he was out hunting with his servants and slaves, and when one of them showed greater hunting skills than Sigi himself, he killed him. For that, he was outlawed, but his father, Odin, helped him escape to a land that would later become Húnaland, a mythological realm that was partly based off the land from which historically the Huns came to Europe. Sigi became the king of this land and reigned peacefully until he was murdered by his wife's brothers. He was later avenged by his son, Rerir.

Sleipnir

At last, we come to our last known demigod in the Norse tradition, and the first nonhuman one in our collection. Sleipnir was a supernatural, eight-legged horse and Odin's steed, and the story of his conception isquit e interesting.

At the beginning of time, not long after the universe was created and the Æsir, or the Norse gods, took their place in Asgard, a mysterious traveler came to their gates offering his services as a builder. He wanted to construct a wall around Asgard, which was definitely a good idea given that the gods would periodically be threatened by different groups of giants. But there was one catch: In return for his work, the builder demanded to be given a wife—and no other than Freyja, the goddess of beauty and love. Moreover, he wanted to obtain the sun and the moon. This was a heavy price to pay.

The gods were torn. They wanted the skills of the builder, but they didn't want to pay the price. So, after some arguing—and being convinced by Loki—they agreed to the stranger's request but put several conditions on him. He was to work alone and had to complete the whole wall in three months. The builder agreed but asked if he could have only one helper, his steed, Svaðilfari. The gods relented.

This turned out to be a mistake. By placing an extremely tight time restriction on the builder, Loki had hoped that the stranger wouldn't be able to complete the work and the gods wouldn't have to pay the price, still getting at least some part of the work done for free. But with the help of Svaðilfari, the builder seemed to be working supernaturally fast. The horse was able to haul enormous rocks and never seemed to tire.

So the gods summoned Loki, blaming him for the situation. It was three days until the deadline, and it seemed that the wall was almost finished. Loki had to come up with a plan, or otherwise, the gods would have to give up Freyja as well as the sun and the moon.

So, on the last night of the building time, Loki, having been threatened with death if he didn't come up with a solution, sneaked upon the wall. As a famous shapeshifter, he turned into a mare in heat. When the builder took Svaðilfari to fetch some more stones for the last touches in the wall, the horse stumbled upon the mare and was immediately drawn to her. He snapped his reins and took off, not heeding the builder's cries. The horses had intercourse and ran together for the whole night, stopping the construction. Thebuilde rdidnot fulfillhisobligat ion.

This caused the rage of the stranger. He revealed himself as a jötunn—a giant from a race hostile to the gods. Sensing danger, the gods called upon Thor, the god of thunder, who defeated the giant by smashing his head with his famous hammer, Mjölnir.

But when the whole affair ended, Loki realized that he had been impregnated by Svaðilfari. He then gave birth to Sleipnir—and so, the ambiguous trickster god became, not the father, but the *mother* of the supernaturalhorse .

Sleipnir was an exceptional steed. Not only could he ride very fast due to his eight legs, but he could also venture into dangerous locations, such as Hel, the Norse underworld for people who didn't die bravely in battle. He could jump over the otherwise impenetrable gate of that unwelcoming place.

One day, Odin rode to the world of the giants, Jötunheimr, and met with a giant called Hrungnir. The giant admired Odin's horse but added that he can bet his horse Gullfaxi would be faster than Sleipnir. This resulted in a mad race in which Hrungnir chased Odin right up to the gates of Asgard, only realizing that he had passed them when he was captured by the gods. Sleipnirw ont he race.

It had been theorized that Sleipnir's role as a horse that could travel between realms corresponds to the shamanic traditions present in Norse culture, especially to that of a shaman and his steed that could carry him beyond the world of the living (Davidson, 2006). In that way, Sleipnir would have an ambiguous status as the intermediary between the worlds—which, given his complicated parentage, is fitting.

Sleipnir closes my short overview of the Norse demigods. In the next chapter, we will venture into the world of the Celts, more specifically, of ancient Ireland, andme et its heroes.

Chapter 3:

Celtic Mythology

The Celtic world consisted of many peoples who, in antiquity, were spread across vast terrains in Europe. Today, the Celtic nations remain only on the British Isles and parts of France—those are the Welsh, Cornish, and Breton on one hand, and Irish, Scottish Gaelic, and Manx on the other. And, contrary to the Norse world and its relatively uniform body of myths, the Celtic world is very diverse. Welsh myths are very different from the Irish, even if they share some characteristics. What is more, it's often difficult to determine the exact nature of characters in those myths. Even though the Celtic culture had been prolific right from the ancient times (giving it antiquity comparable to that of Homer's epic), the myths were only written down during the Middle Ages, mostly by Christian monks who tried to reimagine old pagan gods as human kingsandque ens, or as evil sorcerers.

As a result, it's often difficult to determine which characters in Celtic legends could be interpreted as demigods since the status of their supposedly divine parents is murky. This is especially visible in the Welsh myths. For example, Ceridwen, an enchantress, could be interpreted both as a human woman dabbling with magic and as a goddess of poetry and inspiration. If the latter is the case, then her son, Morfran, and her daughter, Creirwy, would be demigods. But this is not at all certain.

The case is a bit clearer when it comes to the Irish myths, however. They come in cycles—groupings of myths that tie to a certain region of Ireland or a specific time period—and the Mythological Cycle, centered around the stories of a family of Tuatha Dé Danann, is rather clearly based on Irish pagan deities, even if the Christian authors are reluctant to admit it. The Mythological Cycle gives us some insight into the names and stories surrounding the Irish gods, providing us with a clearer view when it comes to heroes descended from them. So, in this chapter, we will focus on two great Irish demigods: Cú Chulainn and DiarmuidO'Dy na.

The Story of Cú Chulainn

Cú Chulainn (also known as Sétanta) is by far the most famous Irish hero and the one for whom we can recreate an almost complete story of his life. A bit like Heracles, he was both a man of supernatural strength andat ragiche ro.

Cú Chulainn's Birth

The conception and birth of Cú Chulainn were miraculous. His mother, Deichtine, was a daughter—or a sister, according to a different version (van Hamel, 1933)—of the king of Ulster, Conchobar mac Nessa.

She was also his charioteer: a warrior woman and a hunter. It was her skill that would bring her to Cú Chulainn's father, Lug, the chief deity in the Irish pantheon and god of warriors and craftsmen.

One day, Conchobar's entourage, including Deichtine, set out to hunt a flock of magical birds who had been eating away all the grass on the ancient hill of Emain Macha, the capital of Ulster. But as the charioteers rode on, snow descended on them, and they were forced to seek shelter.

They found a solitary house in the middle of nowhere. Their hosts were a mysterious man and his wife who gladly took the hunters in, even though the wife was going into labor pains. Deichtine assisted the woman with the birth, and soon, a baby boy saw the light of day.

But when the party awoke after the night spent at the house, they found themselves sleeping in an ancient mound of Brug na Bóinde (today's Newgrange). The house and their hosts were gone, but the boy remained in Deichtine's arms. She decided to take him and raise himashe row n.

But sadly, the little boy soon fell ill and died. Deichtine despaired, but in the middle of the night, the god Lug came to her in her dream. He explained that he had been the mysterious host on that snowy night and that he had put a child in her womb—a reincarnation of the boy.She was supposed to name the boy Sétanta.

But this was only the beginning of Deichtine's trouble. At the time of the miraculous conception, she was betrothed to the warrior Sualtam mac Róich, and when she began showing and it was clear that the child didn't belong to her fiancé, she was suspected of having had intercourse with her own father (or brother), Conchobar.

Deichtine, seeing no way out of the scandal, decided to abort the child. When she was married to Sualtam, she conceived another baby and immediately felt that he was going to be, yet again, the reincarnation of Lug's offspring. When the boy was born, she named him Sétanta. This boy would later grow up and obtain another name—CúChulainn.

From the very beginning, it was clear that Sétanta would be an exceptional boy. Even though Sualtam was considered his father, the child needed foster fathers who would teach him the art of war, good judgment, and an overall education. Several warrior nobles agreed to provide for Sétanta, including King Conchobar. The monarch and his judge and poet, Sencha mac Ailella, were to teach the boy good judgment and eloquence; Blaí Briugu, the wealthiest of the warriors, was to provide food and shelter; Fergus mac Róich, a former king of Ulster dethroned by Conchobar, was to teach Sétanta how to care for and protect the weak and poor; Amergin mac Eccit, the poet warrior of Ulster, took care of his education; and finally, Amergin's wife, Findchóem, was supposed to nurse him. And thus, Sétanta grew up in Amergin and Findchóem's household, along with their son, Conall Cernach. When the boys grew up, they would swear friendship to each other, vowing that whichever of them died first, the other was sworn to avengehimbe forenight fall.

Sétanta's Extraordinary Childhood

Sétanta grew up quickly and displayed extraordinary strength. So, despite his young age, he was allowed by his guardians to join a band of boy warriors who had been training daily at Emain Macha. But they hadn't warned him of a custom that was necessary for his admittance—before running into the training field, he was supposed to ask for the boys' protection.

Sétanta, ignorant of this, ran straight into the field, which was immediately interpreted as a challenge. The boys attacked him, but he defeated them single-handedly. In fact, the ruckus was so great that King Conchobar himself left his hall to intervene. He managed to separate Sétanta from the boys but not before the young hero managed to chase the terrified boys around Emain Macha, demanding that they put themselves under his protection, not the other way around.

Now, the king started paying greater attention to Sétanta. One day, Conchobar was invited to a feast by the royal smith Culann, and as he walked to his house, he passed the training field. The boys were playing hurling—the ancient Celtic game—and Sétanta was among them. The king was impressed by his skill and invited him to come to the feast with him.

Sétanta responded that he would gladly come, but he had to finish his game first. He would join the king later. Conchobar agreed, but when he came to Culann's house, he forgot to mention that fact to the host. Culann had a vicious dog who would tear to pieces any potential intruders, and, as he was feasting with the king,he le t the dog loose as a protection.

When Sétanta arrived at Culann's house, the dog attacked him. In self-defense, Sétanta grabbed the dog and choked him with his sliotar, or hurling ball. Hearing the commotion, Culann and Conchobar went out of the house. Sétanta explained everything, and the king corroborated his story. But Culann was nonetheless distressed by the loss of his precious hound, so Sétanta promised that he would rear him a new one, and until that time, he himself would guard his house. Culann agreed, and from that point onward, Sétanta, as decreed by the royal druid Cathbad, was to be called Cú Chulainn,"Culann'sHound."

Cú Chulainn's Youth and Training

Cú Chulainn's renown grew. Now, armed as he was, he demanded a war chariot from King Conchobar, and the monarch provided him with his own, as it was the only one that could withstand his strength. The first real test to Cú Chulainn's courage—and the first danger to Emain Macha—came in the form of three warrior sons ofanoble manname dNe chtan Scéne.

The three men were set on killing Ulstermen and had boasted that they could kill more of them than were alive. Cú Chulainn rode out of Emain Macha to meet them. He worked himself up to such a battle frenzy that he was killing everyone and everything in sight. Defeating the men was not a problem. But soon, a new issue arose. The Ulstermen were in no danger from the defeated warriors, but Cú Chulainn's frenzy didn't subside. People started fearing that when he returned to Emain Macha, the hero would be dangerous and kill them all.

Conchobar's wife, Mugain, came up with a solution. As Cú Chulainn was riding back to the capital, she led a procession of women who all bared their breasts before him. Even in his battle frenzy, Cú Chulainn was an honorable man, so he looked away and became momentarily distracted. That was the cue for the Ulstermen, and they managed to wrestle him down to a tub of freezing water to cool him down. But the tub exploded from the heat of Cú Chulainn's body, so they put him into another one. The second tub withstood him, but he still managed to boil the water inside. Finally, in the third tub, he cooled down.

This event established Cú Chulainn as the best warrior of them all. It seemed he had no flaws. He was extraordinarily strong, and moreover, very beautiful. Soon, Ulster's nobles became worried that his beauty would seduce all their wives and daughters. They decided that Cú Chulainn's marriage had to be arranged soon—maybe if he turned his eyes to one woman and lovedhe r,ot hers would be safe.

But Cú Chulainn already had one woman in sight. It was Emer, the daughter of Forgall Monach from Lusk (today's County Dublin). But Forgall was opposed to the match; Emer was his younger daughter, and he wanted for his older daughter, Fial, to marry first. Moreover, he disliked Cú Chulainn and thought him dangerous.

So Forgall disguised himself as a prophet king of the Gauls and came to Ulster, suggesting that Cú Chulainn should go away to the Scottish Isles to train under a famous warrior woman, Scáthach. It was Forgall's hope that the trip would prove too dangerous and Cú Chulainnw oulddie .

But Cú Chulainn took up the challenge—after all, his honor was at stake. When he was getting ready for his journey, Forgall sent messengers to the king of Munster, Lugaid mac Nóis, proposing Emer's hand in marriage to him. But the king, having learned that not only Cú Chulainn was fighting for her hand, but also that she loved him in return, refused.

Cú Chulainn was now on his way to Scotland. Scáthach was happy to welcome him among the number of her trainees. She had been training another hero, Ferdiad from Connacht. The two men would soon become best friends and foster brothers. Also, they would share a bed and declare love for each other.

Scáthach not only taught Cú Chulainn everything there was to know about the art of war, but she also gave him supernatural weapons and showed him how to use them. The most prominent of them was a spear called Gáe Bulg, "a spear of mortal pain." It had been made from a bone of a sea monster, and when thrown from the foot at an enemy, it lodged itself so deep in their body that it had to be cut out.

But not all was well during Cú Chulainn's stay at Scáthach's. The warrior woman was attacked by Aífe, her sister and rival, no less fearsome than Scáthach herself. In fact, Scáthach was so worried that Cú

Chulainn would be harmed during the fight that she sneaked a sleeping potion into his food, trying to prevent him from joining. But what was supposed to render him incapacitated for a day and a night, only worked on Cú Chulainn's superhuman body for an hour. When he woke, he heard the commotion from the fight and immediately jumped up to join it. Soon, he was locked in mortal combat with Aífe.

For the first time, Cú Chulainn found his match. Neither he could overpower Aífe nor could she overpower him. But Cú Chulainn had one nonphysical advantage. Before he charged at Aífe, he had asked Scáthach what it was that her sister loved most. Scáthach replied that it was her chariot and her horses. So now, just as Aífe had shattered Cú Chulainn's sword, he cried out, saying that he just saw Aífe's horses runningofft he cliff, taking her chariot with them.

Aífe turned to look, distressed, and lost her concentration. Cú Chulainn immediately overpowered her. Aífe, seeing that all was lost, begged for her life, and Cú Chulainn decided to grant it to her on two conditions: that she stopped attacking Scáthach and that she slept with Cú Chulainn and gave him a son. This, of course, even though Aífe agreed, was rape— and even though, just as Cú Chulainn had hoped, the son he would father with a great warrior woman would be a strong warrior himself, this act would also prove the source of much tragedy in the future.

But now, it was time for Cú Chulainn to return to Ireland. He left Aífe pregnant in Scotland, having given her his ring. She was supposed to give it to her son when he came of age and send him back to Ireland with the condition that he didn't tell his name and parentage to anyone.

When he returned to Ireland, Cú Chulainn continued his pursuit of Emer, but Forgall still refused to give her to him. So he besieged Forgall's fortress, killing many of his men, abducted Emer, and took all the treasure. The couple was married, but in despair, Forgall threw himselffromhisfort ress's ramparts and died.

Tragedy Strikes

Years passed, and Cú Chulainn lived a happy and peaceful life with Emer. He almost forgot about his exploits in Scotland and that somewhere out there, his son with Aífe was growing up. But Aífe didn't forget about the humiliation she had suffered from the hero's hand and how he then left her to pursue another woman. So she brought up her son with Cú Chulainn for the sole purpose of avenging herself. The boy's name was Connla, and he had been trained to never back down from a challenge. He was almost as good of a warrior as Cú Chulainn himself. When he came of age, Aífe sent him to Ireland: She gave him his father's ring, but per Cú Chulainn's own instructions, she forbade him from identifying himself to anyone. The instructions Connla received took the form of *geasa*, ancient Irish taboos that couldn't be broken under the painofac urse.Thus,Connla'sfat e was sealed.

Connla wandered through Ireland far and wide until at last he chanced upon Cú Chulainn's house. His heart beat faster—this was his father's abode. He entered, but

Cú Chulainn, obviously not recognizing him, took him for an intruder. He demanded the boy to identify himself,but Connla,boundby hisw ord,re fused.

Cú Chulainn then attacked him, and they were surprisingly evenly matched. But Cú Chulainn had one advantage: his famous supernatural spear. He hit Connla with it, wounding him mortally. The boy fell to the ground, and from his grip fell the ring, which Cú Chulainn immediately recognized. Stricken with grief, he went to his knees and wept over his dying son. In his last words, the boy said that as two great warriors, together they would have been unstoppable (Meyer, 1904).

Cattle Raid of Cooley

But Cú Chulainn's most famous adventure came when he was only 17, before he killed Connla.

The Cattle Raid of Cooley (an anglicized version of the Irish Táin Bó Cúailnge) was an epic result of a marital disagreement. Queen Medb, an independent warrior queen of Connacht, and her husband, Ailill, were one day comparing their wealth. Medb would be inconsolable if it turned out that her husband was more powerful than her because she had killed men like that in the past. After a thorough debate, it turned out that Medb's and Ailill's wealth was evenly matched, save for one thing—Finnbhennach, an extremely fertile bull. It had been born among Medb's herds but apparently scorned at the fact of being owned by a woman and deserted to Ailill. Medb, enraged, decided that she would obtain an equally fertile bull to match her husband's treasure—Donn Cúailnge from the Cooley Peninsula.

But the farm where the bull was roaming belonged to Ulster. So Medb sent her messengers to try to exhort the bull from its owner, Dáire mac Fiachna. The official message was that she only wanted to rent Donn Cúailnge for a year, but in reality, she never planned to return him. Unfortunately, once the messengers came to Dáire's house and partook in his hospitality, they got drunk and revealed all of Medb's plans to him. Dáire, furious, broke the deal and threw the men out of his house.

But Medb wasn't to be deterred. She soon started raising an army and marched on Ulster. Among her troops were many exiled Ulstermen, including Conchobar's rival and Cú Chulainn's foster father, Fergus mac Róich.

Enter Cú Chulainn, the primary defender of Ulster. Unfortunately, a series of misfortunes befell Ulster on the day of Medb's attack. First, Cú Chulainn was away visiting a woman and didn't see Medb's army. And second, the Ulstermen had been struck by a curse. It was the result of King Conchobar's callousness: One day, he had been participating in a chariot race with the goddess of war, Macha. But the goddess had been heavily pregnant at the time, and yet, Conchobar didn't back off from the challenge. So she now cursed the Ulstermen to experience labor pains for nine days— they were so debilitating that no man could defend Ulster from Medb's army. As a result, she managed to capture the precious bull.

When Cú Chulainn finally realized what was going on, all seemed lost. He was the only defender of Ulster left standing. So he decided to use his wit and went to confront the hostile army at a ford near Emain Macha. It was an ancient custom to invoke a right to single combat at a ford pass, and Cú Chulainn's plan was to defeat Medb's army one by one, day by day, for however long the curse would last. And it would last muchlonge rt hant he initial nine days—months,infac t.

Cú Chulainn stood his ground at the ford, defeating his opponents by day. At night, he was often visited by deities. Another goddess of war, Morrígan, tried to hinder him, but he defeated her; one night, the god Lug came and, revealing himself as the hero's father, healed the wounds on his body. Cú Chulainn slept for three days after that, and during that time, Medb's army slaughtered a bunch of young men who tried to come to the hero's aid. But when he awoke, he was supernaturally transformed by Lug into a fearsome war monster, and he ravaged Medb's army, killing six times moreme n.

After that, the sequence of single combats resumed. Medb sent Fergus mac Róich to fight Cú Chulainn in hopes that she'd break the hero by forcing him to fight one of his foster fathers. But the men made a pact: Cú Chulainn surrendered to Fergus on the condition that Fergus would surrender to him when they met again. Thus,t he odds were evened out.

But Medb had another ace up her sleeve. She managed to capture Ferdiad, Cú Chulainn's companion, best friend and foster brother, and coerced him to fight. Medb's poets threatened Ferdiad that they would describe him as a coward if he refused the challenge—and a poet besmirching one's name was possibly the worst fate that could befall a hero in ancient Ireland.

When Cú Chulainn saw Ferdiad at the ford, he paled. He didn't want to fight the man he loved. He begged Ferdiad to withdraw, but his friend told him about the conditions—it was impossible, a poet's curse was worse than death. So the two friends fought each other for three days, and the odds were even. Finally, Cú Chulainn, having no choice beyond "kill or be killed," thrust his legendary spear at Ferdiad, wounding him mortally. But he himself was too exhausted to fight any longer, and the healers of Ulster carried him away from the ford.

Luckily, it was also the time when the Ulstermen's curse finally started lifting. The men started rising to arms, andsoon,t he climactic battle with Medb began.

At first, Cú Chulainn didn't fight, recovering from his wounds. But when he heard that Fergus mac Róich was cornering Conchobar and about to kill him, he overcame his weakness and entered the battle, confronting Fergus and evoking the earlier promise that his foster father had made him at the ford. Fergus had no choice but to yield. Seeing this, his soldiers withdrew from the battle, and the rest of Medb's army was struck by panic and retreated. The war was won, thanks to Cú Chulainn alone. He even had Medb at his mercy at one point—at the most inconvenient moment, she had gotten her period and had to deal with it—but he refused to kill a defenseless woman.

The conflict, however, left its toll. The bull Donn Cúailnge was never recovered from Medb, and when the queen presented it to Ailill, it killed his bull and was later allowed to roam free. And for Cú Chulainn personally, the victory was bittersweet too because he hadbe en forced to kill his best friend.

Cú Chulainn's Death

Now, it seemed that Cú Chulainn would finally be able to live in peace. But he had many enemies from the past, most prominently Queen Medb, who still couldn't forgive him the humiliation she endured from him in the final stages of the Cattle Raid of Cooley. So she gathered her warriors and conspired. Cú Chulainn was too strong to be killed outright; they first had to weaken his spirit. The only way to do it was to break one of his *geasa*,t he sacred taboos.

One of Cú Chulainn's *geasa* was that he could never eat dog meat. So when one day he was on a journey, Medb sent an old woman to play the role of a host in a house he was staying in overnight. The woman offered Cú Chulainn dog meat. This put him at odds with two sacred rules—that of not breaking one's taboo and that of not breaking hospitality on the pain of a curse. Cú Chulainn had no choice but to eat the meat, and he was greatly weakened.

Then Lugaid, one of Medb's warriors, commissioned three magical spears to be made. It was prophesied that each of the spears would kill a king. Lugaid rode out to meet Cú Chulainn in a combat: first, with the first spear, he killed Cú Chulainn's charioteer, Láeg, the king of charioteers; with the second one, he killed the hero's horse—the king of the horses. With the third one, he mortally wounded Cú Chulainn.

But the hero wasn't dead yet. He didn't want to fall to his knees in a dishonorable way, so he tied himself to a standing stone, facing his enemies and continuing to fight. In fact, Medb's warriors couldn't believe that he was dead until a raven, the sign of death on the battlefield, landed on the hero's shoulder. And even then, when Lugaid came forth, intent on cutting Cú Chulainn's head off as a trophy, the hero's body suddenly emitted a potent ray of light, which cut Lugaid'ssw ordhandoff.

Now, finally, came the time for the childhood oath between Cú Chulainn and his foster brother, Conall Cernach, to be enacted. As you might probably remember, the oath had been that each of the men was to avenge the other's death before sunset. So the moment Conall learned of his foster brother's death, he pursued Lugaid and fought him. Not wanting to be dishonorable, he tucked his right hand into his belt so that he could fight now one-handed Lugaid. The combat was even until Conall's horse bit Lugaid's steed, who then threw him to the ground, killing Lugaid.

Thus ended the life of Cú Chulainn. To this day, he's probably the most recognizable symbol of Irish myth. His supernatural strength was clearly a result of his demigod status, but, like many extraordinary heroes, his life was also marked by periods of tragedy.

Diarmid O'Dyna

Not nearly as famous as Cú Chulainn, Diarmid O'Dyna (an anglicized version of the Irish name Diarmuid Ua Duibhne) is another example of a demigod in Irish tradition. He was a son of Donn, the god of the dead. His mother's name wasn't known, but she was a member of the Fianna—a band of young warriors described in the Fenian Cycle of Irish mythology (a group of legends taking place presumably about 300 years after the events involving Cú Chulainn).

Diarmid was fostered by Aengus mac Óg, the god of love and creativity. He would become the hero's protector, and Diarmid's connotations with love would be the main theme of his adventures.

The Loathly Lady

Diarmid lived with the Fianna: They went together to fight in battles and to hunt, and they occupied the same house. It was a period of aggressiveness and freedom that many young noblemen enjoyed before entering society. And so, Diarmid's life was relatively free of worries—until one freezing night.

It was the middle of winter. The warriors had already gone to bed after an exhausting day of hunting when suddenly an old woman in a tattered cloak and a matted mop of hair on her head entered the hall. She was cold and drenched with rain and snow. She begged each warrior for at least a blanket—but only Diarmid, who was sleeping close to the fireplace, took pity on her and offered her his bed. He, moreover, swore that he would protect her from any attack. The woman was grateful and went to sleep, and Diarmid watched over her. Suddenly, just before dawn, he blinked and couldn't believe his eyes. The woman had transformed from an oldshabby woman to a beautiful young lady.

The woman woke up. She was very grateful for Diarmid's kindness and offered to fulfill his greatest wish. Diarmid instantly asked her to give him his own home that would overlook the sea. The woman agreed, and she led Diarmid to the spot where the house was already standing. Overjoyed, Diarmid instantly asked her to live with him.

The woman agreed; however, there was one condition. He must never mention the lady's state on the first night he met her. Diarmid agreed readily; after all, how difficult could it be? He was capable of a little discretion.

So Diarmid and the woman started living together. The hero's friends grew jealous of his sudden good fortune. They soon came to visit, but Diarmid was out hunting and the lady was watching over his hound and its three pups. Diarmid's three former friends, wanting to partake in some of his wealth, asked the lady to give them one pup each. She agreed—but when Diarmid came home, he wasn't at all happy about this. In anger, he told his new wife that he couldn't believe she could redistribute his own property. Why was she so ungrateful when it was him that overlooked her ugliness ont he first night they met?

Upon these words, the lady looked at Diarmid coolly: He had broken his promise. In a swoosh, she disappeared, and the new house went with her. Diarmid'sbe lovedhounddie dbe forehisve ry eyes.

Very quickly, Diarmid realized his mistake. He set out to search for the lady, wanting to apologize and make things right again. He already suspected that the woman had come to him from the Otherworld—there was no other explanation. So he found an enchanted ship and crossed a turbulent sea to the Otherworld, where he searched through enchanted meadows. At last, he found some inhabitants of the hidden world who told him that the king of their realm had a mortally ill daughter and that she had just come back to him after seven years spent with mortals. Diarmid realized it must be his lady.

He rushed to the lady's side, but she was dying. The only cure that would be available to her was water from a healing cup that was located in the part of the Otherworld known as the Plain of Wonder. But it was heavily guarded by an army of a rival king. Nonetheless, Diarmidvow ed that he would retrieve the cup.

The rival country was divided from the lady's land by an impassable river. It was guarded by a mysterious Red Man of All Knowledge, who had red hair and eyes like coals. Diarmid was not scared of him, so the man helped him cross the river and guided him to the cup.

When the hero announced his intent to the rival king, the monarch sent his champions to meet him in battle. Only if Diarmid defeated them, could he take the cup. But the hero was strong; he beat two times 800 warriors, and when the frustrated king sent new, better troops, he defeated two times 900. The cup of healing was his.

On his way back, Diarmid met the Red Man again. He told the hero how to cure his lady, but he also warned him that when the woman was cured Diarmid's love for her would evaporate.

With a heavy heart, but more intent on curing the lady than on preserving his feelings, Diarmid stood by her bedside and gave her the healing water. As a sign of gratitude, the lady gave him an enchanted ship to return to the mortal lands, and she restored the life of his favorite hound. Diarmid came home to his friends from the Fianna.

This story of Diarmid reads very much like a fairy tale. The next narrative connected to our demigod will also be a romance but of a slightly different kind.

Gráinne

The story of Diarmid and Gráinne started when Gráinne, the daughter of the High King of Ireland, heard that she would be marrying another hero from the Fenian Cycle of myths—Fionn mac Cumhaill. But at the time, Fionn was already old, and Gráinne was disappointed in the match. Still, as an obedient daughter to her father, she couldn't refuse. But she had a plan.

During her wedding feast with Fionn, Gráinne drugged her guests so that they all fell asleep. Only a couple of men remained alert, and Gráinne intended to make her desires known. She first approached Oisín, Fionn's handsome son—but he refused; after all, she was marryinghisfat her, and it would be dishonorable.

Diarmid was next on Gráinne's list. He also refused; Fionn was his leader and friend. Then, Gráinne invoked the power of the gods and imposed a *geas*, a taboo, on the hero that he must follow her. So he left the hall with her amid the laments of his companions. Everyone knew that when Fionn found out about the betrayal, he would kill Diarmid, unheeding of their friendship.

Soon, Fionn awoke. When he heard about what happened, he pursued the fleeing couple. Diarmid and Gráinne hid in the Wood of Two Tents in western Ireland, where they were secretly helped by Diarmid's friends.

Diarmid fortified his abode with a fence containing seven doorways. When Fionn finally found it and besieged it, Diarmid's friends, and even his divine father, Aengus, offered to help him escape through one of the gates—but upon his honor, Diarmid swore that he would do it on his own. He managed to elude Fionn andt ookGráinne with him.

They were now going even deeper into the forest—and farther and farther from the mortal world. At last, they came into the magical center of the woods, where Diarmid defeated a giant who attacked Gráinne. But still, Fionn pursued them and even sent his old nurse, a warrior-woman named Bodhmall, to attack Diarmid. She fired poisoned arrows at him, wounding him and provoking immeasurable pain, but he killed her with his spear.

At last, the god of love and Diarmid's foster father himself, Aengus mac Óg, had to interfere on the couple's behalf. Instructed by the god, Fionn was forced to forgive Diarmid and let him and Gráinne live in peace for several years. But one day, he invited Diarmid on a hunt, where the hero was mortally wounded and even the special healing water gathered in the woods couldn't help him. Diarmid died.

After the hero's death, his father Aengus took his body to his abode in Newgrange where he kept it in a state of perpetual preservation. Whenever he wished to speak to his son, he would breathe a breath of life into his nostrils,re vivinghim.

Thus ended the story of Diarmid O'Dyna. In the next chapter, I will take you into a completely different part of the world. We will learn stories of demigods from various and diverse African traditions, and we'll see how they compare to European ones.

Chapter 4:

African Mythology

Western readers and mythology enthusiasts often make the mistake of assuming that Africa is a uniform entity and that the cultural traditions of various African nations are all the same or similar. But in reality, Africa is a whole continent full of diverse ethnicities and dozens of mythological traditions, all of which would take a separate, long book to exhaust them. Many of those traditions still only exist in oral form and are often difficult to access.

In this chapter, I am going to present to you some chosen demigod-like characters from three different African traditions: from the Nyanga people in Congo, the Mbundu in Angola, and the Hutu, who are interspersed between Rwanda, Burundi, and the Democratic Republic of the Congo.

Nyanga: The Story of Mwindo

The oral story known as the Mwindo epic was first recorded in 1969 by Kahombo Mateene and Daniel Biebuyck (Biebuyck, 1969). It is a story of a magical child from a village of Tubondo named Mwido, who is a son of an evil shaman and the main antagonist of the story, Shemwindo.

Shemwindo decided to take advantage of the fact that among the Nyanga, a father would get a rich gift each time he gave away his daughter in marriage. Shemwindo had seven wives, and, in hopes of getting richer, he ordered that they could only give birth to daughters—anysonw ouldbe executed.

Shemwindo slept with all his wives on the same night, and all of them became pregnant. But the pregnancy of Nyamwindo, the last wife, was especially long and difficult, and she was hindered from any tasks she was required to perform. She feared Shemwindo's wrath, but miraculously, the tasks were being performed without her lifting a finger. This, as it later turned out, was the magic of her son acting from her womb.

Mwindo's birth was equally miraculous. He managed to climb up Nyamwindo's insides and emerged from her middle finger, already bearing his iconic attributes: a scepter, an ax, and a gift from the goddess of good fortuneKahombo:abagc ontainingalongrope .

But soon, Shemwindo learned about Mwindo's birth. He was intent on killing him. First, he threw six spears at him, but Mwindo, already nimble, repelled them with his scepter. Then, Shemwindo tried to bury Mwindo alive, but the boy climbed up using his rope. At last, Shemwindo caught him and sewed him into a leather drum, and then he threw Mwindo into the river. Miraculously, the drum didn't sink, and Mwindo decided to make use of the fact that he was already floating on the river and sailed away, seeking refuge with his extended family—hispat ernal aunt Iyangura.

Mwindo's Journey

Iyangura was married to Mukiti, a hostile serpent spirit. He ordered Musoka, Iyangura's sister-in-law, to block the river. Mwindo, even though he was still in the drum, managed to dig a tunnel under Musoka's body andsw amt ot he other side.

But then, Mukiti himself appeared before Mwindo, blocking the river again. Fortunately, it was already close to where Iyangura was living, and a group of her maidens were gathering water nearby. They dropped their jars and ran to their mistress. Iyangura came quickly and slashed Mwindo's drum open, retrieving the boy.The family was reunited.

But Mukiti was relentless. He wanted to kill Mwindo, and he started plotting against him. As the boy was on his way to his aunt's house, a hedgehog god—Katee— came to him and warned him of the danger. But Mwindo wasn't cowardly, so he decided to go to his aunt's house anyway. Katee dug a tunnel for him so that he could enter the house unobserved.

But Mukiti set traps in the house, each of them full of spikes. The moment Mwindo entered the house, he was confronted with Mukiti's servant Kasiyembe, who challenged him to a dance, hoping Mwindo would trip andfallint oone oft he traps.

Mwindo accepted the challenge. He had another ally up his sleeve: the Master Spider, god of all spiders. He could weave a web so delicate that it was invisible—and so he did, closing all the traps. Mwindo danced to his heart's content and didn't fall.

Now, Mukiti and Kasiyembe called upon their last recourse—the god of lightning, Nkuba. He thrust his spears at Mwindo, but the hero always managed to duck. Then, he used one of the lightning bolts to set fire to Kasiyembe's hair, and when the servant tried to put it out, Mwindo prevented all the rivers from giving himw ater. Thus, Kasiyembe died.

But when Iyangura saw Kasiyembe's lifeless body, she cried and despaired. She asked her nephew to show his power and revive him. Mwindo, taken by her compassion for a rebellious servant, used his magical scepter and waved it over Kasiyembe. The servant came back to life and, grateful for Mwindo's deed, was from then on completely loyal to him.

Back to Tubondo

Now, Mwindo wanted to return to his home village and defeat his evil father. When Iyangura heard about this, she persuaded him to take her and a couple of warriors with him. Also, on their way back, they were to stop at the house of Mwindo's maternal uncle Yana, who was a god of bats and a master smith. Yana had the power of turning Mwindo's body parts hard as iron, as if he were wearing armor at all times.

Yana cut Mwindo into pieces and put them back together, making his skin impenetrable. Thus armed and accompanied by his forces, Mwindo went back to Tubondo.

A battle commenced. At first, only Mwindo's uncles fought with Shemwindo's forces, while Mwindo and Iyangura were watching. But the battle didn't go well; the soldiers were ambushed and only one of Mwindo's uncles barely escaped with his life. It was time for Mwindo to interfere. He entered Tubondo and called for the god of lightning Nkuba, who was now on his side. The moment he raised his scepter into the air, lightning struck the houses in the village, burning them to the ground and killing everyone inside.

Now came the time to take care of his troops; Mwindo revived his uncles with his scepter. Then, he took off to pursue his father who managed to escape the carnage by uprooting a plant and discovering a deep pit that led himint ot he Underworld.

It seemed that Mwindo's journey would now lead farther than just the land of the living.

The Underworld

Mwindo followed Shemwindo down the pit. He fell and landed in the dark jungle of the Underworld, where he carefully followed the path his father had taken. At last, he came to a hut inhabited by Kahindo, the goddess of luck and the daughter of Muisa, the god of the Underworld. Kahindo immediately fell in love with

Mwindo and promised to help him. Unfortunately, she was suffering from yaws, a terrible illness that left sores all over her body. Mwindo helped her wash the sores and brought her a little relief while she gave him advice: He must not accept anything from Muisa—whether it be a seat, food, or drink—lest he'd be forced to stay in the Underworld forever.

The next day, Mwindo stood before Muisa. The god admitted that Shemwindo was in his house, but he didn't agree to betray him to Mwindo unless the young man proved himself to be worthy. He gave him an impossible task—to grow and harvest a banana forest inone day .

Mwindo accepted the challenge. When Muisa heard of this, he tried to hinder him. He sent a magical belt to strangle him, but Mwindo beat it with his scepter. He then beat Muisa himself and gave him the supernaturallyharve sted bananas.

Unsurprisingly, Muisa wasn't placated. He gave Mwindo another task—to harvest honey from his magical honey tree. Even though he was angered by this, Mwindo accepted the challenge. The honey had to be harvested in the early morning, so the hero went to Kahindo's house again to spend the night there. Again, he helped her wash her sores, and when she woke up in the morning, she was completely cured.

Mwindo went to the honey tree and drew the bees out with smoke. But the bark of the tree was hard as rock, and the hero had to call on the god Nkuba again, who struck the tree with his lightning. When one of Muisa's servants saw this, he reported it to his master. Muisa sent his magical belt to strangle Mwindo, but again, Mwindo beat it with his scepter, defeating Muisa. Mwindo gave him the honey, but the god revealed a treacherous truth: Shemwindo wasn't in the Underworld anymore. He had escaped back to the world of the living by a different passage. Mwindo was furious and beat Muisa with his scepter to the ground. Then, having said goodbye to Kahindo, he went back upt ot he mortal land.

Back in Our World

The path that Shemwindo had taken led Mwindo to a giant cave. Unfortunately, it was blocked by Ntumba, the spirit of the aardvark, a nocturnal mammal with a big snout. Ntumba refused to let Mwindo through, and so again, the hero asked for Nkuba's assistance. When the god blew Ntumba up, Mwindo realized that Shemwindo had been hiding behind the aardvark all along. Immediately, Shemwindo started running, and Mwindo pursued him all the way to Great Rift Valley in eastern Africa. The trail stopped there abruptly, and there was only one conclusion—Shemwindo went upwards, into the clouds. Mwindo had no idea how to followhim.

Fortunately, Mwindo soon spotted the giants, who were the children of the sky god Sheburungu, playing nearby. He asked for their help, and they agreed on the condition that Mwindo made them a snack. A small meal for the giants had to be enormous, so Mwindo filled 12 huge wooden bowls with food. The giants were satisfied, and when they finished their meal, they stacked the bowls one on top of the other, making a laddert ot he heavens.

When Mwindo climbed the bowls, he entered the village of Sheburungu. Yet again, the god didn't want to give him Shemwindo unless he performed a task—he had to play a game with him. Mwindo agreed. It was a betting game, so the hero bet all the cattle from his village; he lost. Then, he bet his houses, and lost again. At last, he bet his people, even his mother and his aunt—andlost again.

Something had to be done. In the last act of desperation, Mwindo thumped his scepter on the cloudy ground. The magical weapon then sent its power into Mwindo's hand, and he started winning everything back again. Soon, he wasn't in Sheburungu's debt, but Sheburungu was in his. At last, Mwindo won the sky villageasw ell as his evil father.

But Mwindo didn't want the village. He just wanted Shemwindo. So he graciously gave the village back to Sheburungu while Shemwindo was brought to him in chains.

Mwindo came back to the earth. Even though Muisa now tried to contact him, giving him his daughter's hand in marriage, Mwindo refused. He liked Kahindo, buthadt omarry amort alw omanandrule with her.

Back in Tubondo, Mwindo rebuilt his village and constructed three brass thrones: one for himself and one for his aunt Iyangura. The third one was for Shemwindo. His punishment was of the most educational kind: He would, from now on, sit in chains on the throne and watch his son rule and be a far better chief than he had ever been.

Thus ended the story of Mwindo—a story of a son who was better than his father and of a rebellion and rebuilding of the order.

Mbundu: Sudika-mbambi and Kabundungulu

We are now turning to Angola and the beliefs of the Mbundu people. Sudika-mbambi and Kabundungulu are twin brothers often present in their legends—child heroes connected to thunderstorms and lightning. Through their mother, both boys were grandsons of the Sun and the Moon, which gave them their demigod status. Their father was Kimanaueze, a hero who had to perform a number of difficult tasks in order to obtain the hand of the Sun and Moon's daughter.

Before the boys' birth the Moon had been killed by a vicious monster called *makishi* (perhaps best compared to an ogre) and the boys' ancestral home had been destroyed. But the mother knew that the children she carried would be special and would avenge the wrongs. Even before they were born, they called their mother from her womb, and upon the hour of their birth, they named themselves. They also came out of the womb fully armed. Not long after, they rebuilt their family home.

But it was Sudika-mbambi that, in the end, went out and sought the monsters, while Kabundungulu stayed with his mother. Sudika-mbambi's quest was full of dangers, but he managed to destroy the monster with the aid of supernatural people called the Kipalandes. But those people betrayed him, so he fought with them andw onabride fromamongt hem.

In retaliation for this defeat, the Kipalandes threw Sudika-mbambi into a large hole. He couldn't get out, but he moved some rock and earth around and fell even deeper, straight into the Underworld. There, he met the god of the dead Kalunga-ngombe.

Kalunga-ngombe laid a series of challenges for Sudika-mbambi. If he completed them all, he would be able to take the god's daughter as his second wife. One of the challenges, for example, was to fight a many-headed monster called Kinoka kia Tumba. Sudika-mbambi defeated him, but then, an even more difficult challenge was proposed. He was to fight Kimbiji kia Malenda, a crocodile-like beast. Unfortunately, the crocodile mortally wounded our hero, then swallowed him whole.

And that is when the time came for Kabundungulu to finally shine. When he heard about his brother's ordeal—sensing it through their supernatural bond—he set out on his own journey to the Underworld and rescued Sudika-mbambi from the belly of the beast, then revived him, and healed his wounds. The reunited brothers embraced.

But all was not well. Now, Sudika-mbambi had two wives, while Kabundungulu had none. Kabundungulu asked his brother if he could have one of his brides, but

Sudika-mbambi refused; all brotherly love was gone and they started fighting.

But neither of them could overpower the other. So the brothers decided to part ways amicably—Sudika-mbambi went into one part of the sky, from where he would send thunder to the Earth; and Kabundungulu went to the other part, from where he would echo it.

Hutu: Ryangombe

Our third African demigod hero will lead us to the Hutu tribe in Rwanda, Burundi, and the Democratic Republic of the Congo. Ryangombe has been a powerful ancestral spirit and a subject of a cult in that tribe for several centuries. He is said to be one of the *imana*, semidivine figures—and thus his place in our collection of demigods.

There are numerous versions of his story (Bizimana & Nkulikiyinka, n.d.). Here, I will tell you the most cohesive one.

Ryangombe was a warrior and a ruler who loved to hunt. But when he was about to succeed his father, Babinga, his brother Mpumuti-umucunnyi contested the succession. So Ryangombe proposed a solution: They were to play a sophisticated game of mathematical combinations, and whoever won, would inherit the kingdom.Ry angombelost ,sohe was banished.

On his way from his home, he fought wild animals, among them a serval—a wild cat. After a consultation with an oracle, he then offered the skin of the serval to a young girl he met, and she became his wife. Soon, a child, Binego, was born from this union. According to some versions of the myth, the child spoke to his mother from the womb; according to others, the boy started speaking upon the day of his birth (Bizimana & Nkulikiyinka,n.d.) .

The child grew up very quickly. Soon, he went back to the kingdom of his father and engaged Mpumuti-umucunnyi in the same game that Ryangombe had lost. Ryangombe and his wife followed Binego, and this time, they pointed out the way to win to him. Binego won, and an enraged Mpumuti-umucunnyi tried to pierce him with a spear, but lost. Ryangombe regained his kingdom, commended his son, and made him his officialhe ir.

Ryangombe is said to have been killed by a buffalo that threw him into a tree. It was an *umurinzi* tree, otherwise known for its mystical properties and very bright red leaves. The tree held Ryangombe until he died, becoming a very important element of his cult.

Ryangombe was also said to have established his own cult so that his people, for whom he was a warrior and a champion of their culture, wouldn't forget about him after his death. The initiates of the cult would allow themselves to be possessed by Ryangombe's spirit and recognize his authority over them. One of the purposes of the cult is to recreate the order of the universe established by the spirit of Ryangombe.

Ryangombe closes our overview of demigod heroes from Africa. But we are not leaving the African continent just yet. In the next chapter, I will talk about Egyptian mythology and demigods connected to it.

Chapter 5:

Egyptian Mythology

Ancient Egyptian tradition doesn't have demigods in the most "classic" sense of the word. Egyptian gods rarely had relations with mortals, let alone intercourse with them. But that doesn't mean that ancient Egypt wasn't acquainted with the idea of deified mortals. Spiritually, all pharaohs were the descendants of the gods, and there have been cases of distinguished mortals—mostly the rulers, but not only them—who were deified after death. In this chapter, we will look at two examples of Egyptian approach to deification: first, at a historical figure who became much more after death, and second, at an animal who gained divine parentage.

Imhotep

Imhotep was a chancellor to the pharaoh Djoser from the ancient Egyptian Third Dynasty (in the 27th century B.C.E.). As befitted his role, he was also the priest of the sun god Ra and an architect behind the pyramid of Djoser, the oldest known pyramid in the ancient Egyptian world. Not much else is known, but Imhotep-the-man must have been remembered after his death since almost a thousand years after his death, his name and role started coming back in a completely different context. He became known as a god of medicine, a patron of intellectuals, and an inventor of all stone buildings. Yet his cult was characterized by some distinct differences from the rituals dedicated to other Egyptian gods and goddesses, and that is why the title of a demigod is perhaps most fitting for Imhotep (Hurry, 1926).

Imhotep's cult was unusual. He was a very rare nonroyal figure who managed to attain such veneration. His patronage over medicine might seem surprising. After all, during his lifetime, he had been an architect. But this is most likely due to the transference of some of the features from a different Egyptian god who was a patron of all learning: Thoth. That god was responsible for architecture, mathematics, and medicine. In ancient Egypt, the special, highly qualified cast of the scribes would copy and create texts connected to all three disciplines—and it's most likely due to them that the memory of Imhotep survived.

Although over the years, some medical texts have been, rather dubiously, attributed to Imhotep, there are very few stories about him. Only one of them was preserved, and it's rather late from the 2nd century C.E. In that tale, Imhotep is portrayed as a more typical demigod (probably a result of Greek influence), a son of the god of craftsmen Ptah and a human woman. His sister is identified as Renpetneferet, a minor goddess of youth andbe auty who was also a patroness of the new year.

The story goes as follows: Pharaoh Djoser, Imhotep's master, desired Renpetneferet. But she didn't want him—and yet, he was the pharaoh, so she couldn't refuse him. She begged her brother for help, and he disguised himself—he was a magician—and tried to rescue her. Unfortunately, we don't know how the story ended; the papyrus on which it was preserved only came to us in fragments.

Another fragment of the same papyrus talks about Imhotep's duel with an Assyrian sorceress (Escolano-Poveda, n.d.). During the lifetime of the historical Imhotep, the Assyrian Empire didn't exist yet, but the anonymous author of the story decided to credit the superhero-like figure of Imhotep with battling the Assyrians anyway. In this fragment, Imhotep is also linked to one of the most extensive and famous myths from the Egyptian tradition: the myth about the god of the dead Osiris and how he was killed by his brother Set, who then hacked his body into pieces. In the traditional version of the tale, it is Osiris' wife, Isis, who finds his body parts scattered all around Egypt. But in our story, it was Imhotep who was tasked with retrieving all 42 of them from the Assyrian Empire. After the victorious duel with the sorceress, our hero returned to Egypt and helped Isis bring Osiris back to life.

Imhotep's cult became so prevalent in the later periods of ancient Egyptian history that when the Greeks came upon it, they linked Imhotep with their own god of medicine, Asclepios. He, too, was a demigod and was alsode ifiedaft er death.

Apis: the Sacred Bull

Apis is another example of a nonhuman demigod, or, rather, a deified nonhuman. The cult of a sacred bull in Egypt was tied to the kingship of the pharaoh, and Apis was supposed to be a manifestation of the ruler's strength and courage. But the worship wasn't limited only to images: An actual bull would be chosen every couple of years as an incarnation of the god on earth.

There were several criteria a bull had to fulfill in order to be considered an incarnation of Apis. It was supposed to be black with white markings: a triangular one on its forehead, a mark resembling a vulture's wing on its back, and a crescent moon on its flank. Moreover, it had to possess a scarab-shaped mark underit st ongueandhave double the hairs on its tail.

Such an exceptional bull would then be brought to Memphis, one of the most important religious and political centers in ancient Egypt, and worshiped like a real god—an aspect of Ptah, the god of craftsmen, and a son of Hathor, the motherly sky goddess. He would be given a harem of cows, and his mother would also be treated with honors. It was believed that the special bulls weren't conceived through intercourse, but rather, that their mothers were impregnated through a ray of light coming from the heavens. The behavior of the bull, moreover, would be treated as prophetic, and his movements would be interpreted by priests as the words of an oracle.

After the sacred bull died, he would be buried with honors in the temple complex in Memphis, called the Serapeum. It would be mummified like pharaohs and important officials, and it would be buried standing. The deceased bulls were believed to cross to the Underworld and to protect the pharaohs in their journey after death.

In later years, when the Greek influences on Egypt became quite pronounced, Apis would become linked to one of the most important deities in the Egyptian pantheon, Osiris. As such, he would be depicted in a human form—slightly resembling Zeus—and given a new name, Serapis. Thus, he not only turned from an animalt oagodbut   alsofromabe   ast to a human.

Apis-Serapis closes our quick overview of demigods in Egyptian culture. In the next chapter, we will travel to a completely different corner of the world—to Japan—to meet its heroes.

Chapter 6:

Japanese Mythology

Similarly to other traditions, such as Egyptian and Norse, ancient Japanese tradition doesn't have many demigod characters. The concept of a hero born of a relationship between a god and a human is almost unheard of. However, there are several human figures who have been deified after death, and one who is said, after all, to have descended from the gods. In this chapter, we will look at them closer.

Emperor Jimmu

Probably the closest figure who we would consider to be a demigod, Jimmu was the first legendary emperor of Japan. He is said to have ended the era of the gods and started the era of men. He is believed to have ascended the throne around 660 B.C.E.—however, his historicity is often contested, even though the events he's said to have taken part in might have really happened in one form or another.

Jimmu's father Ugayafukiaezu was said to be descended from the sun goddess Amaterasu, one of the most important deities in Shintoism. Jimmu's mother, on the other hand, had the sea god Ryūjin in her ancestry.

Jimmu and his brothers were born in Takachiho (today's Miyazaki Prefecture on the island of Kyūshū). However, being descended from the gods, they all knew they were destined to rule Japan, so they decided to migrate eastward to find a place from which governing the whole country would be easier. At the time, Jimmu didn't suspect that he would ever become an emperor—he was the youngest of his brothers. It was Itsuse no Mikoto, the eldest brother, who was leading them all on their journey.

Finally, the brothers reached Naniwa (today's Osaka). But it was already occupied and governed by a chieftain, a man with very long legs. A battle ensued, and Itsuse was killed. After the battle, Jimmu realized the root of their misfortune was their army was facing east and had been battling against the blinding sun. So Jimmu led his forces to the other side of the peninsula—next time they would be fighting, they would be facing westward.

This time, a three-legged crow—an embodiment of the sun—guided Jimmu and his people on their journey to Yamato. They battled the local chieftain again, and this time, they won.

Now, Jimmu had to subjugate the whole region. The old chieftain had had vassals—one of them was Nigihayahi, who was also a descendant of the gods. However, when he met Jimmu, he recognized his wisdom and agreed to serve him.

Jimmu was now the emperor. One day, he was surveying his domain, climbing the mountain of Nara. There was an abundance of dragonflies circling around him, and Jimmu observed that the inland sea of Seto, visible from the mountain, was shaped like a heart—incidentally, also similar to a shape that dragonflies made when they were mating.

Suddenly, Jimmu felt a sting on his skin. It was a mosquito that tried to suck in his royal blood. But since Jimmu was the legitimate emperor, and practically a god incarnate, the dragonflies around him attacked the mosquito and killed it. Thus, Japan gained its archaic name: *Akitsushima*, Dragonfly Islands.

Jimmu's reign was said to have been long and peaceful. He died aged 126 and was buried near Mount Unebi in the Nara Prefecture.

The cult of Jimmu has always been present in one form or another in Japan, but it became especially prominent after the so-called Meiji Restoration in 1868—a restoration of imperial rule in Japan. The figure of Jimmu has been since then mostly associated with nationalism and traditionalism, and February 11 was established as a traditional date for Jimmu's ascension to the throne. In the more recent years, the holiday underwent a transformation to the National Foundation Day, a more impersonal holiday associated with the country of Japan rather than a figure of an emperor.

Tenjin

In a way, Tenjin is similar to Imhotep—a historical figure, the scholar Sugawa no Michizane, who was deified after death and made into a deity patron of academics and learning. The historical Sugawa lived from 845 to 903 C.E. and was a revered poet and a politician. He was born to a family of scholars, in fact, the second-highest-ranking family below the emperor. He was the governor of the Sanuki Province, where he was a part of a conflict with an influential clan, the Fujiwara, who feared the immense amount of power he was gaining. This conflict ended with eventual stripping of Sugawa of many of his titles and his being sent to exile, where he died.

But it wasn't his politics that made Sugawa so famous. His poetry, written in both Japanese and Chinese (which was, back then, regarded as a sign of high learning), numbers among one of the most famous examples of poetry from the Heian Period in classic Japanese history.

Sugawa's worship as Tenjin started with a cataclysm. Soon after his death, in 930, the capital of Japan was visited by a series of storms, and lightning killed several members of the Fujiwara clan. This was interpreted as a sign of anger of Sugawa's spirit for the way he had been wronged in his life. To placate the angry scholar, he was posthumously elevated back to his old offices, and the order of his banishment was burned. But that wasn't enough: The emperor also decreed that from now on, Sugawa was to be worshiped as Tenjin, the deity of the sky.

Over time, Tenjin's cult slowly morphed from that of a sky god to a patron of scholars in memory of his lifetime achievements. In his poetry, Sugawa often expressed his love for the *ume* trees (Japanese apricot that blooms with beautiful white flowers), and one of them was even said to have traveled with him into exile. As a result, those trees were often planted around his shrines. In time, Tenjin's role as an angry sky god was completely forgotten, and his fame as a scholar deity was established. To this day, Japanese students pray to Tenjin before their exams, begging for the scholar to lend them some of his wisdom.

Tenjin closes our overview of Japanese demigods. In the next chapter, we'll travel a bit west again—not too much, though. Be prepared to meet the numerous demigods of India and the epic stories attached to them.

Chapter 7:

Hindu Mythology

Unlike many other mythological traditions, the Hindu body of legends and myths abounds in demigods. The two greatest Hindu epics, the *Mahabharata* and the *Rāmāyana*, are full of exploits of heroes who have either been conceived by gods with humans or are incarnations of the gods on Earth. The Hindu belief in reincarnation lends new opportunities to the demigod question.

In this chapter, I will strive to tell you stories of the most prominent demigods in Hindu tradition. There are too many of them to include them all (*Mahabharata* itself is the longest epic poem known to humanity, at over 1.8 million words (Lochtefeld, 2002)). Get ready for stories of epic battles and brave exploits as well as noinsignific antamount oft ragedy.

The Five Pandavas

The five Pandavas were the central heroes of the *Mahabharata*—five brothers and the acknowledged sons of King Pandu from the Kuru kingdom in northern India. Pandu was unable to father children due to a curse, so each of the Pandavas was conceived by a different deity and then acknowledged by the king: Yudhishthira, the eldest, by Dharmaraja, the god of justice and death; Bhima by Vayu, the god of winds and divine messenger; Arjuna by Indra, the sky god of lightning and thunderstorms; Nakula by Nasatya, one of the Ashvins, twin gods of medicine and health; and lastly, Sahadeva, by Darsa, also one of the Ashvins.

Education and Treachery

The five brothers grew quickly and completed their education in the city of Hastinapura. Each one of them was exceptional: Yudhishthira had a spear that could penetrate stone and a war chariot that flew above ground; Bhima was masterful with a mace, and his wrath in battle was so great that it was impossible even for the gods to overpower him; Arjuna was an exceptional shooter and one of the most accomplished pupils of Drona, the brothers' teacher; Nakula was good at fencing and knife-throwing; and Sahadeva fought well with a sword and an ax.

The Pandavas completed their studies alongside their cousins, the Kauravas. But there was no love between them. Especially, Bhima would often play pranks on the cousins and engage in wrestling matches, where, being supernaturallyst rong,he would often overpower them.

This wasn't to the liking of the oldest of the Kauravas, Duryodhana. He wanted Bhima dead and even poisoned his food—and when Bhima was incapacitated, he tried to drown him in a river. Thankfully, Bhima was saved by a serpent-god Vasuki, who also bestowed upon him the strength of 10,000 elephants.

But Duryodhana wasn't done with his hatred. He feigned repentance, but in secret, he was planning another calamity. He built Lakshagriha, a palace coated with highly flammable lacquer, and invited the Pandavas, along with their mother Kunti, for a visit. He was planning to burn them alive.

Luckily, the prime minister of the Kuru kingdom, Vidura, overheard Duryodhana talking about his devious plan to his counselor, Purochana. He warned the brothers while they were entering the palace—there was no time before the whole place would be on fire. In order not to raise Purochana's suspicion, Vidura used a different language, only understood by the Pandavas.

So Bhima, the strongest of the bunch, grabbed his brothers and his mother and carried them out of the palace through a secret tunnel. He then barred the doors from the outside. Duryodhana wasn't inside at the time, but Purochana was, so he got his comeuppance.

Because the fire consumed everything, Duryodhana and his hundred brothers the Kauravas didn't know that the Pandavas were still alive. So Kunti gathered her five sons and suggested that they live together incognito until the danger passed. They traveled together to West Bengal, where they lived for a time in a little village.

Pandavas in Hiding

This was the time of the first significant exploits of all the five Pandavas. Bhima defeated a demon called Bakasura, who had been eating the inhabitants of the village in which the brothers were staying. Incidentally, the demon had been born during the same cosmic phase as Duryodhana, so that day, a prophecy was born that one day Bhima would kill his cousin just as he killedt he demon.

At this time, the brothers also encountered another demigod, the princess Draupadi. I will talk about her in more detail in the latter part of this chapter; here, let's just focus on how she came to be involved in the Pandavas' life.

She was exceptionally beautiful, and her father established a contest for her hand. It was an extremely difficult shooting contest, in which the candidates had to shoot through the eye of a golden fish only looking at its reflection in the water. But since Arjuna was a master archer, he succeeded.

That, however, wasn't to the liking of other contestants. All of them were powerful kings and princes, and Arjuna had competed incognito, dressed as a Brahmin (a member of the cast of priests). So the other men attacked Arjuna, but they were no match for him. He defeated them and, excitement still coursing through his veins, ran home to his mother to announce his success.

However, in his excitement, he failed to explain precisely what happened. "Mother, look what I've found!" he cried, and Kunti, assuming this was some precious object Arjuna had chanced upon, responded, "Then you must share it with your brothers as has always been the case."

This was an unlucky misunderstanding. Kunti's words in that moment had the power of a vow. Besides, it had been agreed before that the oldest of the brothers, Yudhishthira, should marry first. So Arjuna was forced to share his new wife with all of his five brothers: a rare example of a marriage where there were more grooms than there were brides.

The brothers agreed upon the rules and limitations of this unusual agreement. If any of them wished to spend the night with Draupadi, the others were forbidden from interrupting on the pain of a year of celibate exile. Later, the brothers would also find other brides, but Draupadiw asalw ays their chief consort.

The Great Return

After a time in hiding, the Pandavas decided to return to Hastinapura. Unfortunately, Duryodhana was still alive, and soon a conflict arose between him and Yudhishthira over which one of them should be the crown prince of the Kuru kingdom. Yudhishthira had been the crown prince before because he was older, but after his supposed death in fire, Duryodhana was crowned. Duryodhana's father, Dhritarashtra, went for advice to the commander of his forces, Bhishma, and he advised him to divide the kingdom in half and give the one half to Yudhishthira and his brothers. And so, the Pandavas were given their half, where they built a magnificent city of Indraprastha. Yudhishthira was then crowned the prince of that city.

He now had to perform a special ritual called Rajasuya—a sacrifice to mark his consecration as king of Indraprastha. All of Yudhishthira's brothers then traveled to all corners of the kingdom to gather tribute fort he sacrifice.

Bhima went east to the Magadha empire and battled its supernatural ruler, Jarasandha, for several days. The odds were even, and although in the end Bhima managed to overpower Jarasandha, he couldn't kill him. Sohe aske dLordKrishna,t he chief god, for help.

Krishna showed him the way to kill Jarasandha by taking a twig, cutting it in half, and throwing both halves in the opposite directions. And so, Bhima did the same with Jarasandha: He cut him in half and separated the two halves so that the body of his opponent couldn't rejoin.

Now, Bhima had the empire subdued, and he released Jarasandha's prisoners. The emperor had held a hundred kings in his dungeons, and now, they all became the supporters of Bhima and the Pandavas.

Meanwhile, Nakula went west. He subjugated several kingdomsaft er a series of battles.

Sahadeva went south. He was skilled with a sword, and it was widely believed that the Southerners were good swordmasters. He defeated a number of kingdoms, real and legendary, such as the cannibals reportedly living by the seacoast.

But Arjuna's march north was interrupted. As he was preparing for his travel, he entered the royal palace to collect his arms—and inadvertently stumbled upon Yudhishthira having a dalliance with Draupadi. The rules were clear: Arjuna had to go into exile for a year. Even though Yudhishthira tried to dissuade him from that—it had been an accident, after all—Arjuna was adamant.

Arjuna's travels during his exile led him through many places. Even though he stayed true to his word, he didn't respect all the elements of the Draupadi pact. He didn't stay celibate, but instead, had no fewer than three marriages. He also formed a deep bond with Lord Krishna.

The Game of Dice

But despite the Pandavas' political success, Duryodhana's hatred for them wasn't quenched. So, with the help of his advisor and friend Prince Shakuni, he devised another plot: He invited the brothers to his palace to play dice with them. But it wasn't just an ordinary game. Shakuni had magical dice that always played as he wished them to. It wasn't difficult to see where all this would lead.

Duryodhana started playing with Yudhishthira. Soon, the eldest brother lost all his riches, including his magnificent city and all the lands his brothers had conquered for him. He wanted to stop playing, but Duryodhana and Shakuni taunted him and his honor. Yudhishthira had nothing else to put as a bet—that is, apart from his own brothers. So he did just that and lost again. At last, he could only bet himself—and again, he lost .

The game seemed over. But Duryodhana was devious. He said that Yudhishthira could still bet his wife Draupadi, and if he won, Duryodhana vowed to give hime verything back. Yudhishthira, tricked, agreed.

Of course, he lost Draupadi, too. Duryodhana, triumphant, ordered the former empress to be brought to him as a slave. To the shock of everyone assembled, he had her stripped of her clothes, boasting that a slave girl had no rights and couldn't complain. Even though everybody was astonished by Duryodhana's cruelty, nobodyint ervened.

But Draupadi didn't want to be disgraced. She prayed to Lord Krishna to save her, and he heard her prayer. He made her sari to be of infinite length so that when Duryodhana tried to unwrap it, he couldn't get to Draupadi's skin, instead finding layers upon layers of clothing. Frustrated, at last he gave up.

Seeing this divine intervention, Duryodhana's father, King Dhritarashtra, feared that Draupadi had the power to curse his sons, the Kuravas. So he walked up to the former empress, apologized, and released her as well as the Pandavas.

Duryodhana couldn't endure this. He threatened his father with suicide if he didn't agree to him playing with the Pandavas one last time. This time, the rules would be different. The loser would have to spend 13 years in exile, and the last year would have to be completely incognito. If the cover was blown, another 13 years would have to be endured. Dhritarashtra, though at this point frustrated with his son's unstable behavior, didn't want to lose him, so he ordered the Pandavas to play.

Unsurprisingly, since Duryodhana still had the magical dice, he won this time, too. The Pandavas had to go into exile—but they knew that the problem of Duryodhana would have to be solved once and for all. They were going to use their 13 years to prepare for war.

The Exile and the War

The Pandavas spent their exile in the Matsya Kingdom in northern India, disguised as peasants and serving King Virata. During that time, they prepared for war. Arjuna spent the time winning magical weapons from the gods, while the other brothers made a last effort at negotiating with Duryodhana. But all was futile—a war was on its way.

The war lasted 18 days and was extremely bloody. All 100 Kauravas were slain, and their army was slaughtered, even as the Pandavas' army also suffered big losses. But as was prophesied, Bhima killed Duryodhana.

In the end, Yudhishthira was crowned king, and the brothers were back to their good graces. It is said that they ruled Hastinapura in peace for 36 years.

The End

At some point during the Pandavas' reign, Lord Krishna left the mortal earth. This, in Hinduism, marked the beginning of Kali Yuga—the last of the ages of the world and the worst one. The five brothers and Draupadi understood that their time had come to its end; they needed to be liberated from the hardships oflife through death.

So they set out on their last journey: to climb Mount Kailash (today's Tibet). They were accompanied by a dog,w how asYama—t he god of death— in disguise.

On their way up to the summit, Draupadi suddenly slipped, falling down a cliff, and died. It happened because of her imperfection—she had loved Arjuna more than her other husbands. Next came Sahadeva: He had been too confident, too sure that he knew everything when it came to science. After that, Nakula slipped: He had been too vain when it came to his looks. Then, Arjuna died, his imperfection being that he was too proud of his military exploits. Next came Bhima, who had been too brutal when dealing with his enemies.

At last, only Yudhishthira was left. He alone managed to reach the gates of Svagra Loka—heaven. When he entered, none of his brothers, nor Draupadi, were there.

Instead, none other than... Duryodhana was sitting on ac elestial throne.

Panicked, Yudhishthira asked Yama-the-dog for an explanation. The god said that Duryodhana, along with all his brothers, died valiantly in battle and, therefore, were allowed into Svarga Loka. The Pandavas and Draupadi,ont he other hand, had their imperfections.

But all was not lost. They were now in hell, repaying their debt from life, but it was only temporary, and eventually, they would join Yudhishthira in Svarga. The eldest brother then demanded to be brought to hell to see his wife and his brothers.

Yama complied. Hell was terrible—full of carnage, fire, and gore. Yudhishthira barely restrained himself from running away, but when he heard the cries of his loved ones, he braced himself. He announced to Yama that he would accompany his wife and brothers in their penance—he preferred to spend a time in hell with goodpe ople than a time in heaven with his enemies.

Yama smiled. Suddenly, the curtain fell, and they were all in heaven again. The god explained that this had all been an illusion designed to test Yudhishthira and to purge him from the last of his imperfections. In reality, all his loved ones were in heaven. And thus, the story of the Pandavas ended in a happily ever after.

Draupadi

A lot of Draupadi's story has already been told as closely tied to the Pandavas. But there are still some gaps: Why was she considered a demigod, and who was shebe foreshe me t the five brothers?

Birth by Fire

To meet Draupadi's parents, we have to move to the kingdom neighboring Kuru, Panchala. Before her birth, her father, King Drupada, was defeated by Drona, the teacher of the Pandavas, and lost half his kingdom. He wanted vengeance—but none of his allies were strong enough to defeat Drona. So he decided to perform a fire sacrifice, called *yajna*. He wanted to have a strong sonw how ouldave ngehim.

The sacrifice was given and the ritual was performed, after which the priests ordered Drupada's wife, Queen Prishati, to eat the offerings. She responded that she wasn't ready; she first had to wash herself. But the priests couldn't wait—one of them took the offerings andpoure dt hem onto the fire.

Suddenly, from the flames, a beautiful pair emerged: a man and a woman. The woman, especially, was enchanting, with her dark complexion and eyes like lotus flowers. Immediately, a prophecy was spoken: The woman—Draupadi—was to be the first of all women, and her life was to mark the destruction of the Kauravas.

The twins accepted the parentage of Drupada and Prishati and agreed to live with them in their palace. They were given names: Dhrishtadyumna and Draupadi. Dhrishtadyumna would later become the ally oft he Pandavas and one of their commanders.

As soon as Draupadi became of age, her father organized a *svayamvara* for her, which is a ceremony in which a husband was to be chosen. We know the rest of the story—how Arjuna won the contest and how then Draupadi became a wife of all five Pandavas due to a misunderstanding. It's clear in the *Mahabharata* that she admired all of the brothers, even though she might havelove dArjunat he most.

Insulting Duryodhana

From the time when Yudhishthira established his capital and performed his Rajasuya, we have a story that explains why Duryodhana hated Draupadi not only as the Pandavas' wife but in her own right.

Duryodhana was visiting the Pandavas' palace. It was a magnificent structure, and there were many magical illusions hidden all over its grounds. Unluckily, Duryodhana fell for one of those illusions, which resulted in him suddenly finding himself waist-deep in a hiddenpool,w et and splattering water.

Draupadi and her maids saw this from a nearby balcony. Draupadi laughed and, reportedly, said, not quite kindly, that "the blind man's son is blind" (Ravi, 2020). King Dhritarashtra, Duryodhana's father, was blind. Duryodhana, understandably, was enraged by this andsw oreve ngeance.

The Exile

It is said that during the Pandavas' exile, Draupadi was abducted by Jayadratha, Duryodhana's brother-in-law. He used the brothers' absence on a hunt to take her. First, he tried to persuade Draupadi to go with him willingly, but when she refused, he grabbed her and put her into his chariot. But the Pandavas very quickly learned about this and pursued Jayadratha. Seeing this, he abandoned Draupadi on the road, trying to save his skin.But he was caught nonetheless.

The brothers now deliberated what to do with him. Draupadi, unsurprisingly, wanted him dead, but Arjuna pointed out that Jayadratha had a close relationship with King Dhritarashtra, and they had to spare him. Draupadi was upset by this; the incident created the onlyrift there ever was between Draupadi and Arjuna.

During the 13th year of the Pandavas' exile—the one they were supposed to spend incognito—Draupadi disguised herself as a servant and served Sudeshna, the queen of Matsya. Kichaka, Sudeshna's brother, seeing a beautiful servant in the palace, lusted after Draupadi and asked for her hand in marriage. Of course, she refused. She said she was already married to celestial beings—she couldn't explain whom.

But Kichaka persuaded his sister to help him win Draupadi. So, the queen created an opportunity for a meeting, sending Draupadi to fetch some wine. On her way to the winery, Kichaka cornered and assaulted her. She managed to escape and quickly ran to Virata, Sudeshna's husband and king of Matsya. Kichaka pursued her, and, when already in the court, he kicked her in front of everyone, including the Pandavas who hadbe en disguised as courtiers.

This was a grave insult. Virata didn't react, and only a look at Yudhishthira prevented Bhima from interfering. Draupadi, feeling helpless and insulted, cried out, asking Virata if he thought he was a good king, allowing an insult such as this to go unpunished. She then turned to Kichaka and cursed him, saying that he would die at oneofhe rhusbands'hands.

Kichaka laughed. "Where are those legendary husbands?" he asked. So far, Draupadi had failed to provide their names.

The exchange was interrupted by Yudhishthira. He said that Draupadi should go to a temple because she was safe from Kichaka there. She exchanged a meaningful glance with him and went.

Now, Draupadi and the Pandavas devised a plan. She agreed to pretend that she had changed her mind and fell in love with Kichaka. In his pride and folly, he wouldn't realize that it was fake. She would then say that she'd marry him on one condition—that none of his family and friends would know about their union. Then,she would invite him to a dancing hall at night.

And so it happened: Kichaka fell for Draupadi's words immediately, and when he came to the dancing hall,

Bhima was already waiting for him. Kichaka's mutilated body was then shown to his family, and Draupadi pronounced that it was one of her celestial husbands who did this.

Angered, Kichaka's brothers forced Draupadi to be tied to his funeral pyre. But Bhima, yet again, saved her, killinge veryone around them.

Here end the stories of Draupadi. She's a rare example of a woman who had many husbands and was not shunned for it—even if it did arise from a misunderstanding. She also displayed some amount of agency, which makes her something more than just a complimentary character to the Pandavas.

Karna

Our next demigod will bring us to the opposite side of the divide between the protagonists and antagonists of the *Mahabharata*. Karna was a loyal friend of Duryodhana, but he was also a half brother to the Pandavas, a fact that he had not been aware of from the beginning. Thus, he is a tragic hero who ends up fightinghisow nfamily .

Birth and Parentage

But let us start from the very beginning. Karna's mother was Kunti, later the mother to the Pandavas—but back in her teenage years, she went by the name of

Pritha. She was a daughter of King Shurasena. One day, a seer and scholar visited Shurasena's court, and Pritha made sure that he had everything he needed during his stay. Grateful for this, the seer gave Pritha a mantra (a prayer), telling her that if she spoke it, she could ask any godt ogive he rac hild.

Pritha used the mantra the very next day, out of curiosity if anything else. She called for the god of sun Surya. And it worked: Surya conceived a child with her. But now, Pritha had another problem. She was unmarried, and she was scared that her miraculous pregnancy would cause a scandal. So she concealed it, and when the child was born, she put it into a basket andse nt it adrift on a river.

But the child didn't die. Through a series of rivers, the basket eventually reached the shores of the Ganges and found its way to ancient Bengal. Radha, a charioteer's wife, was passing the river when she spotted the basket with a crying child in it. She took pity upon it and took it home to her husband, Adhiratha Nandana. The pair namedt he boy Karna and raised him as their own.

But when it was time for the boy to go to school, Radha told him the truth about the day he was adopted. Karna felt ashamed that his parents must have abandoned him, and it informed his self-worth throughout his life.

School

Karna was sent to school in Hastinapura, and he studied under the warrior Drona, among others. In fact, he was a student at the same time when his half brothers, the Pandavas, went to school—of course, nobodykne w the truth.

During his time at the school, Karna was often bullied due to his supposed lowly parentage. The *Mahabharata* portrayed his psychological profile very well. He was lonely due to his peers' bullying; at the same time, he was ambitious and excelled in study and piety as well as showed compassion to those in need. But his low self-worth often meant that he would brag too much about hismart ialskills(McGrath, 2004).

Duryodhana would turn out to be the first real friend of Karna during his school time. His motives might have been selfish since he primarily befriended Karna when he saw that he matched his peer Arjuna in his archery skillsandw anted to have an ally against the Pandavas.

And soon, Karna's usefulness for Duryodhana came into play. An archery contest was announced, and Duryodhana pushed Karna to compete against Arjuna. But there was a catch. Before the contest started, the rivals had to announce their lineage. If Karna announced his charioteer parentage, he would not be allowed to compete against noble Arjuna. So Duryodhana stepped in, announcing that he was about to anoint Karna as the king of all Bengal.

Karna was overwhelmed. He asked Duryodhana what he wanted in return for the kingdom. But Duryodhana only responded with a smile that he wanted Karna's unendingfrie ndship.

The anointing ceremony came. Karna invited his adoptive parents, for which he was ridiculed by the Pandavas; Bhima even called him "dog-like" (McGrath, 2004). For that, Karna would never be able to forgive the Pandavas.

During the ceremony and, later, the archery competition, everyone still laughed at Karna. Only Duryodhana didn't renounce him but, instead, took his hand as a sign of friendship in front of everyone. He would, from now on, become Karna's most precious friend as well as mentor. Karna would help him scheme against the Pandavas, even though his motives for overthrowing them were different, and much more legitimate, than those of Duryodhana.

However, even as he took part in Duryodhana's schemes—such as the famous game of dice and the subsequent humiliation of Draupadi—Karna was never proud of himself afterwards. He was always quick to angerbut equally quick to regret.

The Tragic Discovery

But there came a day when all of Karna's life would turn upside down.

It was already far into the cycle of violence and rivalry between the Pandavas and Duryodhana. After the brothers went into exile, Lord Krishna came to Karna's Bengal court and announced himself. Karna received him, and the god said that he wished to end the cycle of violence that was tearing the land apart. He then revealed Karna's true parentage—his mother was Kunti and that technically made him the eldest of the Pandavas. He could use this knowledge and become king and, thus, unite the conflicted sides. He could make the Pandavas serve him and take Draupadi as a wife.

Karna reeled at this information. He said that he didn't consider himself the son of Kunti; it was Radha who really brought him up and loved him. Therefore, she was his real mother. Moreover, he already had a wife and children, and all that was thanks to his adoptive father Adhiratha, who he regarded as his real father. He didn't want power; it was love that counted.

So Lord Krishna left Karna and went to Kunti, persuading her to come and meet Karna. When she did, Karna received her cooly, introducing himself as the son of Radha and Adhiratha. He accused Kunti of abandoning him and reiterated what he had said to Lord Krishna about love being more important than blood ties. Kunti apologized for her behavior—but also begged Karna not to fight his half brothers. Karna responded that he had made a vow to Duryodhana—he would fight on his side. He would not kill four Pandavas, but Arjuna, who had been his staunchest enemy since school, would have to die. Kunti left in tears.

The Final War and Death

On the eve of the final battle between the forces of the Pandavas and Duryodhana, Arjuna and his divine father Indra hatched a plan. Since Karna had been fathered by Surya, he was immortal—he had magical earrings and a breastplate that protected him from death. Arjuna wanted to rob him of those—so Indra disguised himself as a beggar and asked Karna for his protective gear as alms. Karna was very pious, so he gave away his immortality in the name of alms. He had to cut the marks of immortality off his body, thus literally stripping himself of his gift.

Indra was taken with Karna's extraordinary generosity. In return, he gave him a missile that could kill anyone, no matter if mortal or immortal. Of course, Karna plannedt ouse the missile on Arjuna.

But the war revised these plans. In the end, Karna ended up using the missile on Bhima's son, Ghatotkacha. That took away his advantage over Arjuna.

Then, Karna ended up in a combat with Arjuna. The duel was evened out until Karna's chariot got stuck, and the hero became distracted when he tried to fix his wheel. Arjuna then dealt him a fatal blow.

Karna is perhaps the most sympathetic hero of the *Mahabharata*. He is a victim to circumstance, and his motivations are completely understandable. His piety and his views on family come across as very likable and fresh, even if he participates in his friend Duryodhana's evil schemes.

Hanuman

The last Hindu demigod in our selection will bring us to another important Indian epic, the *Ramayana*. Hanuman is a central character, and he mostly doesn't interact with the heroes from the *Mahabharata*—that is, apart fromBhima.

Hanuman is an unusual hero. He is a humanoid monkey, and, unlike the heroes I've already talked about, he is worshiped as a god. His patronage includes wisdom, strength, courage, devotion, and self-discipline.

Hanuman's mother, Anjana, had originally been a water spirit. But due to a curse, she was born on earth as a mortal princess. One day, Anjana was praying to Vayu, the god of wind. At the same time, in a remote corner of India, King Dasharata was performing a ritual that would grant him children. The gods looked kindly on the king and gave him a sacred pudding to share between his wives so that they would conceive. But as Dasharata was carrying the pudding to his spouses, a bird snatched a portion of it and quickly flew away. The bird later dropped the pudding over the place where Anjana was praying. It was Vayu who delivered it safely to Anjana's hands, and when she ate it, she became the mother of Hanuman, while Vayu was his spiritual father.

Hanuman's Childhood

One of the most famous stories connected to Hanuman happened in his childhood. One day, he saw the red sun setting over the horizon. It looked like a ripe fruit, and Hanuman was hungry. So he jumped up and snatched the sun from the sky.

The king of the gods Indra didn't like this. As a punishment, he struck Hanuman with his thunderbolt, and the young monkey fell dead on the spot. This, in turn, was not to Vayu's liking, and he took away all the air and wind from the Earth. Everything was dying. At last, Lord Shiva revived Hanuman. The monkey gave back the sun, and in turn, he became supernaturally strong.

That didn't mean he became responsible, though. Like a proper trickster, Hanuman would use his powers to prank people—until one time, he unwittingly made a sage the butt of his joke. The sage, enraged, cursed him to forget his powers. And so, Hanuman entered adulthoodignorant ofhist ruest rength.

Adult Adventures

Hanuman was in service to the god Rama. He was sent on a mission: to retrieve the god's kidnapped wife, Sita. He was accompanied by a whole array of supernatural beings, including Jambavan, the king of bears.

The group reached the ocean and wanted to sail to Sri Lanka. But none of them could swim, and they couldn't jump as far as the horizon either. That is, Hanuman could, but he didn't remember. Then Jambavan, who remembered rumors about Hanuman's previous exploits, asked Hanuman why he couldn't use his powers. In a flash, Hanuman remembered: The curse was lifted.

So Hanuman enlarged himself and flew across the ocean. In Sri Lanka, he shrunk to the size of an ant so that he could penetrate the capital city, which was occupied by demons. It wasn't long until Hanuman found Sita guarded by demons. He waited until night fell and had a secret conversation with her. She told him that the king of the demons had kidnapped her and was forcing her to marry him.

Hanuman said that he was going to rescue Sita; however, she refused, faithful to an ancient Indian belief that only a husband could do such a deed (Pai, 1971). Angered, Hanuman started destroying everything around him. Soon, the demons woke up and captured him,t hen brought him before the king himself.

The king taunted Hanuman and ordered for his tail to be set on fire. But every time they tried to cover the tail with a cloth soaked in oil, it grew longer. At last, the king had enough of this and ordered the tail to be lit anyway. Hanuman quickly shrunk his tail again and broke from his bonds, and then he jumped out of the window. His tail was burning, and he ran from roof to roof,light ingt he whole city on fire.

Hanuman managed to escape Sri Lanka. When he came back to Rama, he related everything that happened, and the god started preparing an army to retrieve his wife.

Hanuman became a general, and for his many deeds of valor,he was rewarded by Rama with immortality.

Encounter With Bhima

And that is how Hanuman survived up until the events of the *Mahabharata*, which took place centuries after the *Ramayana*. Hanuman was now living in the forest, nearly forgotten. But one day, Bhima—also the son of god Vayu, and thus, Hanuman's spiritual brother—was passing through. When Hanuman saw him, he immediately knew who he was: the strong Bhima who liked to boast about his supernatural strength. Hanumande cided to teach him a lesson.

He lay down in the middle of the road, pretending to be a frail old monkey. When Bhima approached, he asked him to move because he was blocking his way. But Hanuman refused, explaining he was too weak. Bhima couldn't step over him—it would be very rude. So Hanuman suggested that Bhima could lift his tail to create a passage for him. Bhima agreed, but when he grasped the tail and tried to lift it, it wouldn't budge. Suddenly, it was heavier than all the weight of the world combined.

Bhima blushed in shame. He realized that this was no ordinary monkey and asked Hanuman to reveal his true nature. Hanuman did, and Bhima realized they were spiritual brothers. They hugged and, from then on, would be the fastest of companions.

After the events of the great war of the Pandavas, Hanuman disappeared again and wouldn't be spotted fort he next couple of centuries.

Chapter 8:

Other Traditions

Our selective overview of mythologies by no means exhausts the list of known demigods. I wanted to devote this last chapter to three heroes from other, perhaps lesser-known traditions, as an example of what other cultures have to offer. Consider it your invitation to more exploration.

Ancient Mesopotamia: Gilgamesh

The *Epic of Gilgamesh* is the oldest known epic in the world (Andrews, 2018). It's not often recognized that its titular character, Gilgamesh, the king of Uruk, was a demigod according to the story. Although he might have been a historical monarch (having ruled somewhere between 2900 and 2350 B.C.E.), in the story, he is presented as a man with superhuman properties, and he was most likely worshiped as a deified human after death.

The *Epic of Gilgamesh* describes him as only one-third mortal (Powell, 2009). His mother, Ninsun, was a titular goddess of the city of Uruk and a patroness of wild cows, while his father, Lugalbanda, was a mortal king who would later, like Gilgamesh, be deified after death.

Moreover, Gilgamesh's creation seemed to have been a group effort: Shamash, the sun god, gave him beauty, while Adad, the god of the storm, endowed him with courage.

Enkidu and Gilgamesh's Character Development

When Gilgamesh came of age and became the king of Uruk, he was a tyrant. He was brutal, forced his subjects to perform labors for him, and most likely even abused his power for sexual favors. So the king of the gods Anu decided to enact a corrective punishment for Gilgamesh: He created a wild man, Enkidu, who was destined to come to Uruk and challenge the king.

Enkidu challenged Gilgamesh to a wrestling match. Gilgamesh won, but he was impressed not only by Enkidu's strength, which almost matched his own, but also by his courage. Gilgamesh's behavior immediately changed; he became fast friends with Enkidu. There is also some evidence in the poem suggesting that they were lovers (Mehlhorn, 2016).

Now, Gilgamesh and Enkidu went out for a series of epic adventures. First, they went to the Cedar Forest: in Mesopotamian mythology, the realm of the gods. It was guarded by Humbaba, a supernatural king. He barred the passage to Gilgamesh and threatened him; the hero was so terrified that he prayed to the god Shamash, who blew his wind into Humbaba's eyes. Blinded, the king begged for mercy—but Gilgamesh and Enkidu decapitated him anyway. Then, they destroyed the forest.

Interestingly, a few years ago, a new fragment of the *Epic of Gilgamesh* was unearthed (Tharoor, 2015). It describes the rather brutal act in which Gilgamesh and Enkidu engaged not as an example of prowess, but as an incident that could anger the gods and which Gilgamesh then regretted. In this version, Humbaba, too, isn't shown as a primitive, monster-like figure but asasophist icated foreign king with an elaborate court.

After their adventure, Gilgamesh and Enkidu returned to Uruk. There, Gilgamesh was confronted by Ishtar, the goddess of love, who demanded to become his queen. But he wasn't on board with that proposal; the goddesshadt reated her former lovers poorly.

Enraged by the refusal, Ishtar sent a mighty Bull of Heaven to attack Uruk. But Gilgamesh and Enkidu killed it and made a sacrifice to Shamash of its heart. Ishtar, not wanting to give up, stood by the walls of Uruk and cursed Gilgamesh. He scorned her and ordered a celebration for the defeating of the bull while Ishtarmourne dit sde mise.

But Ishtar's curse wasn't spoken in vain. Soon, Enkidu had a dream in which the gods pronounced their verdict: Both Gilgamesh and Enkidu would die as a punishment for killing the bull. Not long after, Enkidu hadanot her dream in which he saw the Underworld.

Enkidu soon grew sick. His death followed not long after. Gilgamesh couldn't be consoled. For days, he wept over his friend's body and refused to accept his death and bury him. When he finally did, the ceremony was long and elaborate, and Gilgamesh composed a beautiful poem for his friend.

Gilgamesh's New Journey

Enkidu's death shook Gilgamesh's whole world. It not only bereaved him but also reminded him of his own mortality. Gilgamesh found himself scared of death. So he undertook another journey, which would be his quest for immortality. He went to the home of Utnapishtim, the only survivor of the Great Flood (most probably the same cataclysm that was described int he Bible).

The journey to Utnapishtim's house abounded in minor adventures. Gilgamesh killed lions. Then, he met a magical scorpion-man with his wife, who, hearing of the reason for the hero's journey, allowed him to progress instead of blinding him with their light. Then, Gilgamesh wandered through darkness for 12 days until, at last, he came to the light where he met Siduri, who brewed beer for the gods. She also guarded an immortalgarde n.

At first, Siduri tried to persuade Gilgamesh to turn back and accept his mortality. But he refused, so, resigned, she let him pass. The next stop on the journey was the ferry across the sea by Urshanabi, the ferryman of the gods. Only then, Gilgamesh finally reached Utnapishtim's house.

The hero was exhausted. But as soon as he met Utnapishtim, the man told him that in order to become immortal, he had to refrain from sleeping. Gilgamesh tried, but in the end, failed. He fell down and was asleep forse ven consecutive days.

Utnapishtim woke Gilgamesh. He told him that not all was lost—he couldn't be immortal, but he could still regain youth. All he had to do was to use a special plant. It wasn't difficult for Gilgamesh to find it—but yet again, he failed when he went for a swim in a river andle ft the plant on the shore. A snake stole it.

Dejected, Gilgamesh decided to return to Uruk. Immortality was impossible for a man, even if he was a descendant of the gods.

The Epic of Gilgamesh, as it survived to this day, doesn't have much else to say about Gilgamesh as many fragments have been lost to time. But still, the surviving part tells us enough of a moving story about a man who turned from a tyrant to a loving companion and about a human'sst ruggle with the concept of mortality.

Ancient Assyria: Semiramis

Semiramis is another semilegendary character who might have been a historical ruler. Her character is partly based on a real queen named Shammuramat (ca. 850–ca. 798 B.C.E.), who controlled vast terrains from the Caucasus to the Arabian Peninsula. It's also worth bearing in mind that the accounts about Semiramis don't come from the Assyrians themselves but from their neighbors, primarily the Greeks. Thus, her figure is often exoticized and purposefully portrayed as strange.

The first account of Semiramis comes from a Greek historian called Diodorus Siculus (1st century B.C.E.). According to him, Semiramis' mother was Derketo, an Assyrian fish goddess, who paired with a mortal king to produce such great offspring (Beringer, 2016). But Derketo abandoned Semiramis soon after her birth, and the little girl was raised by doves.

One day, a shepherd who worked for the royal court found a child playing among the doves. He took her to the king, and from then on, she was raised at the court asone oft he ladies-in-waiting.

When Semiramis was of age, she married a royal general called Onnes. Soon, people around her discovered that she had a great talent for battle strategy, and she became the advisor to King Ninus. At some point during one of the numerous Assyrian wars, the city of Bactra was besieged; not only did Semiramis give sound advice on how to gain it, but also she led a platoon of warriors and captured a strategic point, which then led to the capture of the city.

Ninus was now so awed by Semiramis that he begged Onnes to give her to him as a wife. But Onnes refused; he loved his wife. So the king offered his own daughter as a replacement, but still, Onnes refused. Then Ninus decided to use his kingly power. He threatened Onnes with blinding if he didn't comply. Onnes, fearing the king and unable to give up his love for Semiramis, hanged himself. After a short period of mourning, Semiramis and Ninus were married.

They had a son together—Ninyas. One day, during the conquest of Asia, King Ninus was gravely wounded and couldn't lead his troops into battle. So Semiramis disguisedhe rselfasNiny asandle dasuc cessful attack.

All in all, Semiramis' reign over the Assyrian Empire was supposed to last 42 years (Beringer, 2016). She was said to have conquered and upheld large terrains, and even though nominally only a king's wife, she seemed to have ruled in his stead.

Over the ages, Semiramis' portrayal changed. From the mostly positive pre-Christian depictions, praising her prowess, she started to be viewed as a promiscuous and corrupted queen by the medieval Christian writers. In the end, she almost became a symbol of decay (Beringer, 2016).

Polynesia: Māui

At last, we are briefly jumping into a completely different mythological tradition—Polynesia. The character of the cultural hero Māui is present throughout the region, from the islands of New Zealand, through Hawaii, Tongo, Tahiti, Samoa, Mangareva, and others. Depending on a region, there are different versions of the Māui myth: Here, I will cite some examples of his exploits.

According to the Hawaiians, Māui was the son of Hina, the sea goddess. He was a trickster right from the beginning, and one day, his trickery became the origin story behind the creation of the Hawaiian Islands.

Māui, even though he was the youngest of his brothers, persuaded them to take him out fishing. But instead of trying to catch a fish, he lodged his hook in the ocean bed. The fishing rod strained. Seemingly, Māui had caught a great fish. He convinced his brothers to paddle so that they could take it out. They did and were so preoccupied by their effort that they didn't notice a largeislandrisingfromt he water behind them.

Another legend is tied to Māui's role in changing the course of the day. Once upon a time, days were much shorter than they are now; the sun moved way faster on the sky. Hina, Māui's mother, complained to him that she couldn't even manage to dry her clothes when she emerged from the sea before the day's end. So Māui climbed the massive volcanic island Hale-a-ka-lā and made a lasso out of his rope. He caught the sun and forced it to go slower.

In the Māori mythology of New Zealand, Māui was the son of a woman named Taranga and the king of the Underworld, Makeatutara. The child was born prematurely and his mother thought he was going to die, so she threw him into the ocean wrapped in leaves. But Māui was found by ocean spirits, who wrapped him in a protective layer of seaweed and laid him on the shore. There, he was found and raised by his grandfather. When he came of age, he returned to his family home where he met his brothers who, though initially mistrustful, accepted him in the end, especially after they saw his shapeshifting abilities.

Māui also met his mother. He became very attached to her and didn't want her to leave him ever again. But she would always go out just before dawn and come back at night, and Māui had no idea where she went. So one day he followed her, disguised as a bird—and it turned out that she went to the Underworld to see her husband. After she saw Māui follow her, she finally recognized him as the son she had once abandoned.

Among Māui's exploits, apart from slowing down the sun and the creation of islands, was also something very important: bringing fire to the humans. In those days, humans couldn't make fire by themselves, but instead, they had to ask Mahuika, the goddess of fire. Māui, who incidentally, was a grandson of Mahuika, offered that he would go to the end of the world, where she lived in a largevolc ano,andw ouldst eal the fire from her.

The fire came from Mahuika's fingertips. When Māui met her, she told him that she could give the fire to the humans and that he could take it from one of her fingertips. But Māui wasn't satisfied by that. One by one, he extinguished the fire from all of Mahuika's fingers until he angered her. She hurled a fireball at him, and he transformed into a hawk to run away. She was, in fact, so angry, that she set almost all of the islands on fire, and Māui had to ask the god of weather Tāwhirimātea and the goddess of thunder Whaitiri-Matakataka to extinguish it. They did, but not fully; Māui brought the remaining fire to his village, and then he taught the humans how to rub dry sticks together in ordert olight the fire.

Conclusion

We have now reached the end of our journey. It was an epic one! Through time and space, we met heroes, heroines, and sacred animals. By now, you have probably noticed the sometimes uncanny similarities between characters from different cultures and time periods. Most of the demigods were characterized by superhuman strength and extraordinary cunning—but some of them were also haunted by tragedy. The lives of Heracles, Achilles, Cú Chulainn and Karna often showed that a hero's life could be eventful but short and marked by sorrow. On the contrary, other demigods, such as Māui, Jimmu, Mwindo, or Ryangombe, would become cultural heroes and overcome the obstacles on their path, teaching humanity new skills, for which they would be forever revered. We have met "traditional" demigods—half-humans, half-gods—and we have met deified mortals. We even met a quite large menagerie: the supernatural horse Sleipnir, the sacred bull Apis, and the divine monkey Hanuman. The world of the demigods is definitely richer than just a few famous names.

But this isn't the end. By necessity, this book was a selection of stories—there are countless other demigods out there, not only within the cultures mentioned in this book, but others, perhaps more obscure or underrated. And so, it is my hope that after reading this book, you will be inspired to search for more stories and characters. If the selection I presented to you teaches us anything, it is that, despite their superhuman qualities, the demigods are sometimes very… human. For the people who told their stories, they were what fantasy characters are to us today: extraordinary and magical, but also relatable and sympathetic. I hope you found them so as well.

References

Abrantes, M. C. (2016). *Themes of the Trojan Cycle.* Coimbra.

Adekunle, J. (2007). *Culture and customs of Rwanda.* Greenwood Press.

Andrews, E. (2018, August 23). *What is the oldest known piece of literature?* History Channel. https://www.history.com/news/what-is-the-oldest-known-piece-of-literature

Anthon, C. & Smith, W. (2010). *A new classical dictionary of Greek and Roman biography, mythology and geography: Partly based upon the dictionary of Greek andRomanbiograph yandmyth ology.*K essinger.

Apollodorus & Hard, R. (1998). *The library of Greek mythology.* Oxford University Press. (Original work published 1921)

Aston, W. G. & Barrow, T. (1998). *Nihongi chronicles of Japan from the earliest times to A.D. 697; two volumes inone .*Tut tle Publishing.

Beringer, A. L. (2016). *The sight of Semiramis.* Acmrs Publications.

Biebuyck, D. (1969). *The Mwindo epic.* University of CaliforniaP ress.

Bizimana, S. & Nkulikiyinka, J. B. (n.d.). *Le culte de Ryangombe au Rwanda.* https://www.africamuseum.be/sites/default/fil es/media/docs/research/publications/rmca/o nline/documents-social-sciences-humanities/ryangombe.pdf

Borgen, R. (2021). *Sugawara no Michizane and the early Heian court.*Unive rsity of Hawaii Press.

Buck, W., Nooten, V., & Triest, S. (2019). *Mahabharata.* University Of California Press.

Dalley, S. (2008). *Myths from Mesopotamia creation, the flood, Gilgamesh and others.*OxfordUnive rsity Press.

Davidson, E. (2006). *Gods and myths of the Viking age.* Barnes&Noble Publishing.

Dronke, U. (1969). *The Poetic Edda.* Oxford University Press.

Escolano-Poveda, M. (n.d.). *Imhotep: A sage between fiction and reality.* American Research Center in Egypt. https://www.arce.org/resource/imhotep-sage-between-fiction-and-reality

Euripides & Allan, W. (2013). *Helen.* Cambridge University Press. (Original work published 1891)

Euripides, Davie, J., & Rutherford, R. B. (2004). *Electra and other plays.* Penguin Books. (Original work published1891)

Eusebius. (2008). *Chronography* (R. Bedrosian & A. Smith, Trans.). Topos Text. https://topostext.org/work/531 (Original work published1818)

Graves,R.(2017). *The Greek myths.*P enguin Books.

Grimal, P. (2000). *The dictionary of classical mythology.* Blackwell.

Gantz,J.(1981). *Early Irish myths and sagas.*P enguin.

van Hamel, A. G. (2017). *Compert con Culainn, and other stories.*Trie ste Publishing.

Herodotus. (2015). *The histories book 2: Euterpe.* Simon andSc huster. (Original work published 1849)

Highfield, R. (2007). How Imhotep gave us medicine. *The Daily Telegraph.* https://www.telegraph.co.uk/news/science/sci ence-news/3293164/How-Imhotep-gave-us-medicine.html

Hollander, L. M. (1945). *The skalds, a selection of their poems.*The Ame rican-Scandinavian Foundation.

Homer, Murray, A. T., & Wyatt, W. F. (2003). *Iliad.* Harvard University Press. (Original work published1924)

Homer, Butcher, S. H., & Lang, A. (2010). *The Odyssey.* Seven Treasures Publications. (Original work published1882)

Hurry,J.B.(1926). *Imhotep*.Sandpipe rBooks.

Kapoor, S. (2002). *The Indian encyclopedia: Biographical, historical, religious, administrative, ethnological, commercialands cientific*.CosmoP ublications.

Kitagawa, J. M. (1987). *On understanding Japanese religion*. Princeton University Press.

Leeming, D. A. (1998). *Mythology: The voyage of the hero*. OxfordUnive rsity Press.

Lindow, J. (2002). *Norse mythology: A guide to the gods, heroes, rituals, and beliefs*.OxfordUnive rsity Press.

Lochtefeld, J. G. (2002). *The illustrated encyclopedia of Hinduism*.Rose n.

Lucian of Samosata, Hayes, E., & Nimis, S. A. (2015). *Lucian's dialogues of the gods: An intermediate Greek reader*.F aenum. (Original work published 1905)

Lynch, P. A, & Roberts, J. (2010). *African mythology A to Z*.Che lseaHouse .

Mcgrath, K. (2004). *The Sanskrit hero: Karṇa in epic Mahābhārata*.Brill.

Mehlhorn, D. (2016, February 11). *Homophobia: A modern sickness*. Medium. https://medium.com/@DmitriMehlhorn/hom ophobia-a-modern-sickness-c41763f94bca

Meyer, K. (Ed.). (1904). The death of Connla. *Ériu, 1*.

Morales, M. S. & Mariscal, G. L. (2003). The relationship between Achilles and Patroclus according to Chariton of Aphrodisias. *The Classical Quarterly*, *53*(1), 292–295. https://doi.org/10.1093/cq/53.1.292

O'Grady, S. H. (1857). *Toruigheacht Dhiarmuda Agus Ghrainne, or The pursuit after Diarmuid O'Duibhne and Grainne, the daughter of Cormac mac Airt, king of Ireland in the third century.* The Ossianic Society. https://play.google.com/store/books/details?i d=16sDAAAAQAAJ&rdid=book-16sDAAAAQAAJ&rdot=1

Pai, A. (1971). *Hanuman*.AmarChit raKat haP vt Ltd.

Pepin, R. E. (2008). *The Vatican mythographers.* Fordham University Press.

Pinch, G. (2002). *Handbook of Egyptian mythology.* Abc-Clio.

Plutarch, Dryden, J., & Clough, A. H. (1992). *Plutarch: The lives of the noble Grecians and Romans.* Modern Library.(Originalw orkpublishe d1683)

Powell, B. B. (2009). *Classical myth*.P rentice Hall.

Quintus De Smyrne & Hopkinson, N. (2018). *Posthomerica.* Harvard University Press. (Original work published 1891)

Ravi, J. N. (2020, May 19). *Did Draupadi insult Duryodhana during Rajasuya, Karna in Swayamvara?* My India My Glory.

https://www.myindiamyglory.com/2020/05/1
9/did-draupadi-insult-duryodhana-during-
rajasuya-karna-in-swayamvara/

Rose,H.J.(2013). *Ah andbookofGre ek mythology, including
its extension to Rome*.Ke ssingerP ublishing.

Ross, M. C. (2011). *A history of old Norse poetry and poetics*.
D.S.Bre wer.

Sandars, N. K. (1982). *The epic of Gilgamesh*. Penguin
Books.

Sappho & Chandler, R. (1998). *Sappho*. Everyman.
(Original work published 1733)

Schlauch, M. (1964). *The saga of the Volsungs: The saga of
Ragnar Lodbrok, together with the lay of Kraka*.
American-Scandinavian Foundation.

Sturluson, S. & Anderson, R. B. (2017). *Prose Edda*.
Digireads.com.

Suzuki, M. (1992). *Metamorphoses of Helen: Authority,
difference, and the epic*.Corne llUnive rsity Press.

Talbert, C. H. (1975). The concept of immortals in
Mediterranean antiquity. *Journal of Biblical
Literature*, 94(3), 419.
https://doi.org/10.2307/3265162

Tharoor, I. (2015). A new chapter in the world's oldest
story. *Washington Post*.
https://www.washingtonpost.com/news/world

views/wp/2015/10/06/a-new-chapter-in-the-worlds-oldest-story/

Valmīki, & Goldman, R. P. (2016). *The Ramayana of Valmiki: An epic of ancient India. Volume V, Sundarakanda.*P rinceton University Press.

Walcot, P. (1984). Greek attitudes towards women: The mythological evidence. *Greece and Rome, 31*(1), 37–47. https://doi.org/10.1017/s001738350002787x

Westervelt, W. D. (1910). Legends of Ma-ui: A demigod of Polynesia, and of his mother Hina. *Hawaiian Gazette.*

Williams, G. M. (2016). *Handbook of Hindu mythology.* MotilalBanarsidass.

Made in the USA
Middletown, DE
21 March 2023